Art of
Organisational Management

Published by :
Lotus Press Publishers & Distributors

Art of Organisational Management

A.K. Banerjee

Lotus Press

4735/22, Prakash Deep Building
Ansari Road, Darya Ganj,
New Delhi - 110002

Lotus Press : Publishers & Distributors
Unit No. 220, 2nd Floor, 4735/22, Prakash Deep Building,
Ansari Road, Darya Ganj, New Delhi- 110002
Ph.: 23280047, 98118-38000
• E-mail : lotuspress1984@gmail.com
www.lotuspress.co.in

Art of Organisational Management

ISBN: 978-81-8382-212-1

Printed & Published by : **Lotus Press Publishers & Distributors,** New Delhi-02

PREFACE

Organisational management refers to the techniques, art and principles which go into the process of managing an organisation. The field is vast one, considering especially the complex range of activities that the term comprises-organisational behavior, finance, marketing, human resource, etc. With the pervasion of the commercial field in nearly very field of life, corporatisation has come about to establish itself an inevitable reality of our lives, marked by intense competition and struggle. Management thereby, with its whole range of techniques to enable a business enterprise to succeed and thrive, has become an indispensable part of a business organisation.

The present text is an effort to guide readers towards comprehending what organisational management is all about, characterised as it is by the cut-throat competition and the struggle for making profits and maintaining a company. The book seeks to guide readers on what it means to e a manager in the contemporary scenario, and what is meant by the art of organisational management in a comprehensive manner. Supplemented with various case-studies, the book seeks a pragmatic approach towards management rather than a theoretical one.

It is hoped that the incisive contents of the book serve well for all. Any suggestions for further improvement are most welcome.

Editor

CONTENTS

1

MANAGEMENT APPROACHES

Management covers a wide variety of activities. Theorists and academic authors have contributed to the study management and one can see a huge volume of writings on the management. The various approaches to management and umpteen number of differing views have only added to the confusion of what the management is all about. It isn't surprising to know that a highly respected author had called the situation as "the management theory jungle".

VARIOUS APPROACHES TO MANAGEMENT

Analysis of management from various view points have to led to different approaches. They have been summarised as below:

Empirical/case Approach

Characteristics: Knowledge based on experience through case studies. Analyses successes and failures.

Limitations: No concrete principles of limited value for developing management theory.

Group Behaviour Approach

Characteristics: Importance on people as groups and their

behaviour. Study of Social and Organisational Behaviour of the people in groups.

Limitations: Generally differs with management concepts, theories and techniques. Closer integration with organisation structure is needed.

Cooperative Social Systems Approach

Characteristics: Concept includes any cooperative group with a purpose and is concerned with both interpersonal and group behavioural aspects.

Limitations: This approach overlooks the managerial concepts and is too broad a field for the study of management.

Interpersonal Behaviour Approach

Characteristics: Concentrates on interpersonal behaviour, leadership, motivation and human relations.

Limitations: This approach too like the earlier ones ignores managerial concepts such as relations, planning, organising and controlling.

Systems Approach

Characteristics: According to this approach, unlike the earlier ones management concepts such as planning organising and controlling are given due importance. Interaction with the external environment is also considered.

Limitations: There is nothing new about this approach to the management.

Socio-technical Systems Approach

Characteristics: Technical systems such as production and office operation have great effect on social system such as personal attitudes and group behaviour.

Limitations: This concept places importance on labour and lower-level office work and ignores other managerial knowledge.

Mathematical Approach

Characteristics: In this concept managing is treated as a mathematical processes. It is viewed as a purely logical process and is expressed in mathematical symbols and relationships.

Limitations: Managing is not a pure science and hence cannot be completely modelled.

Mckinsey's 7-s Framework

Characteristics: The seven S's are 1. Strategy, 2. Structure, 3.Systems, 4. Style, 5. Staff, 6. Shared values and 7. Skills.

Limitations: Though the concept is of practical value, the terms used are not discussed in detail.

Contingency Approach

Characteristics: Managing different situations and circumstances is influenced by the organisational behaviour.

Limitations: There is no one answer to a problem. There can be more than one best way to do a thing. Calls for creativity and can be very complex.

Operational Approach

Characteristics: This approach draws concepts, techniques and knowledge from other fields and managerial approaches. Distinguishes between managerial and non-managerial knowledge.

Limitations: Does not, as some authors say, identify "coordination" as a separate function.

Decision Theory Approach

Characteristics: Focuses on making of decisions and decision-making process.

Limitations: This concept is too bounded i.e. either it is too narrow and at times it is too wide. Management consists of more than making decisions.

Managerial Roles Approach

Characteristics: Original study consisted of observations of only five chief executives.

Limitations: Sample was very small and some activities considered are not managerial.

SYSTEMS APPROACH TO MANAGEMENT

Just as human body is formed of different interdependent systems so is also an organisation. A change in any one of these systems may affect all or some other systems to varying degrees. This 'ripple effect' influences the effectiveness of the organisation. To understand the interactions and the consequences between the various systems of the organisation the managers should posses the ability to get a perspective view. Treating an organisation as formed of different systems is known as systems approach.

Systems theory was first applied in the fields of science and engineering. It also has found wide acceptance in the practice of management. A system can be defined as essentially a set or assemblage of things interconnected or interdependent, so as to form *a complex unity.* Cars, computers, television and radio sets are some examples of systems.

There are two major types of systems: Closed and Open. A closed system has definite boundaries; it operates relatively independently and is not affected by the environment outside the system. Stand by generator is an example of a closed system. With its different systems working together in perfect harmony the generator continues to supply power as long as it has sufficient fuel supply without much regard to the external environment.

An open system as the name implies, is characterised by its interaction with the external environment. Clearly, any business or other organisation must be described by an opensystem model that includes interactions between the enterprise and its external environment.

One important mechanism which makes the system to adapt and adjust to the changing conditions of its environment and to exercise control over its operations is 'feedback'. As explained thus far, systems approach of management provides an integral approach to management. It views management in its totality. It helps in seeing the problems of the organisation in wider perspective. This approach is more useful in managerial decision-making.

Based on the systems approach, Talcot Parsons has suggested three meaningful levels in the hierarchy of complex organisations: Technical, Organisational, and Institutional.

The Technical Level is concerned with the actual production and distribution of products and services. It also includes activities like research and development, operation research and accounting.

The Organisational Level coordinates and integrates work performance at the technical level. It is concerned with obtaining the continued flow of inputs into the system and maintaining the markets for the outputs from the system.

The Institutional Level is concerned with relating activities of the organisation to environmental system. It involves relating the organisation to the needs of the environment.

Social Responsibilities of Management

According to Keith Davis, "Social responsibilities refer to the businessman's decisions and actions taken to reasons at least partially beyond the firm's direct economic or technical interest". To quote Andrews, "By social responsibility, we mean intelligent and objective concern for the welfare of society that restrains individual and corporate behaviour from ultimately destructive activities, no matter how immediately profitable and leads in the direction of positive contribution to human betterment variously as the latter may be defined".

The concept of social responsibility is not new. Although the idea was already considered in the early part of the 20th century, the modern discussion of social responsibility got a major impetus with the book *Social Responsibilities of the Businessman* by Howard R. Bowen. he suggests that business managers are bound to "pursue those policies, to make those decisions or to follow those lines of action which are desirable in terms of the objectives and values of our society". In other words businesses should consider the social implications of their decisions. As one may expect, there is no complete agreement on the definition of social responsibility. A survey conducted on the matter revealed "Corporate social responsibility is seriously considering the impact of the company's actions on society".

2

MANAGERIAL DECISION-MAKING

A managerial function that encompasses all the other functions of management, that is, making decisions.

- A decision is a choice made from available alternatives.
- Decision-making is the process of identifying problems and opportunities and selecting a course of action to deal with a specific problem or take advantage of an opportunity.
- Managers often are referred to as decision makers.
- Managerial decision-making differs from personal decision-making in the systematic, specialised attention that managers give to decision-making.
- Decision-making is not easy. It must be done amid ever-changing factors, unclear information, and conflicting points of view.
- Good decision-making is a vital part of good management, because decisions determine how the organisation solves its problems, allocates resources, and accomplishes its goals.
- Although many of their important decisions are strategic, managers also make decisions about every other aspect of an organisation, including

structure, control systems, responses to the environment, and human resources.

- Plans and strategies are arrived at through decision-making; the better the decision-making, the better the strategic planning.
- Managers scout for problems and opportunities, make decisions for solving or taking advantage of them, and monitor the consequences to see whether additional decisions are required.
- Decision-making deals with problems. A problem arises when an actual state of affairs differs from a desired state of affairs. Examples of problem situations are:
  - A deviation from past experience.
  - A deviation from a set plan.
  - Other people's problems or decisions.
  - The performance of competitors.

In many cases, a problem maybe an opportunity in disguise.

It is not always clear whether a situation faced by a manager presents a problem or an opportunity. David B. Gleicher, a management consultant, defines a problem as something that endangers the organisation's ability to reach its objectives, and an opportunity as something that offers the chance to exceed objectives.

According to Peter Drucker, opportunities rather than problems are the key to organisational and managerial success. Drucker observes that solving a problem merely restores normality, whereas the exploitation of opportunities leads to progress.

TYPES OF MANAGERIAL DECISIONS

The first classification of personal and organisational

decisions was suggested by Chester Barnard in his classic book: *"The Functions of the Executive"*. In his opinion, the basic difference between the two decisions is that "personal decisions cannot ordinarily be delegated to others, whereas organisational decisions can often, if not always, be delegated'.

Thus, a manager makes organisational decisions that attempt to achieve organisational goals and personal decisions that attempt to achieve personal goals. Personal decisions can affect the organisation, as in the case of a senior manager deciding to resign.

Another common way of classifying types of decisions is according to whether they are basic or routine Basic decisions are those which are unique, one-time decisions involving long-range commitments of relative permanence or duration, or those involving large investments. Examples of basic decisions in a business firm include plant location, organisation structure, wage negotiations, product line, etc. Most top management policy decisions can be considered as basic decisions.

Routine decisions are the everyday, highly repetitive management decisions which by themselves have little impact on the overall organisation. However, taken together, routine decisions play a tremendously important role in the success of an organisation. Examples of routine decisions include an accounting entry decision and a salesperson's decision on what territory to cover.

Finally, most management decisions typically fall into one of two categories: Programmed and Non-programmed.

Programmed decisions involve situations that have occurred often enough to enable decision rules to be developed and applied in the future. Programmed decisions are used for dealing with recurring organisational problems, whether complex or uncomplicated.

If a problem occurs repetitively and routinely, and a specific approach can be worked out for handling it, then it may be a candidate for programmed decision-making.

— Programmed decision-making is relatively simple and tends to rely heavily on previous solutions.

— Programmed decisions limit freedom because managers have less latitude in deciding what to do.

— However, programmed decisions save time and cost less, allowing managers to devote attention to other, more important activities.

— Lower-level managers essentially confront familiar and repetitive problems; therefore they most typically rely on programmed decisions such as policies, standard operating procedures, and rules.

— Examples of programmed decisions are inventory of a given product to be maintained, salary range of a newly hired employee, and handling of customer complaints poorly defined and largely unstructured, and have important consequences for the organisation.

— Non-programmed decisions deal with unusual or exceptional problems.

— If a problem has not come up often enough to be covered by a policy or is so important that it deserves special treatment, it must be handled as a Non-programmed decision.

— Also, when a manager confronts an ill-structured problem, a custom-made, Non-programmed response is required.

— Most of the problems that top managers of an organisation confront are non-recurring and ill-structured. Hence, as a manager moves up the organisational hierarchy, the ability to make Non-programmed decisions becomes important.

— Deciding whether to acquire another organisation or to sell off an unprofitable division, deciding which markets offer the most potential, or deciding how to allocate an organisation's resources are examples of Non-programmed decisions.

— Another classification of decisions relates to:

- Complexity of the problem in terms of the number of factors associated with it.
- The extent of certainty that can be placed with the outcome of a decision.
- Based on these two dimensions, four kinds of decision modes can be identified: Mechanistic, Analytical, Judgemental, and Adaptive.

— A mechanistic decision is one that is routine and repetitive in nature.

— It usually occurs in a situation involving a limited number of decision variables where the outcomes of each alternative are known.

— Most mechanistic decision problems are solved by habitual responses, standard operating procedures, or clerical routines.

- In order to further simplify these mechanistic decisions, managers often develop charts, lists, matrices, decision trees etc.
- An analytical decision involves a problem with a larger number of decision variables, where the outcomes of each decision variable can be computed.
- Management science and operations research provide a variety of computational techniques

like linear programming and statistical analysis that can be used to find optimal solutions.

— Many production and engineering problems are complex, but solutions can be found.

— A judgemental decision involves a problem with a limited number of decision variables, but the outcomes of decision alternatives are unknown.

— Many marketing, investment, and resource allocation problems come under this category.

— Good judgement is needed to increase the possibility of desired outcomes and minimise the possibility of undesired outcomes.

— An adaptive decision involves a problem with a large number of decision variables, where outcomes are not predictable.

— Because of the complexity and uncertainty of such problems, decision makers are not able to agree on the nature or on decision strategies.

— Such ill-structured problems usually require the contributions of many people with diverse technical backgrounds.

— In such a case, decision and implementation strategies have to be frequently modified toaccommodate new developments in technology and the environment.

— Decision-making under different states of nature:

— Every decision situation can be organised on a scale according to the availability of information and the possibility of failure.

— The four positions on the scale are certainty, risk, uncertainty, and ambiguity.

— Decision-making under certainty occurs when a manager knows the precise outcome associated with each possible alternative or course of action.

- In such situations, there is perfect knowledge about alternatives and their consequences.
- The probability of specific outcomes is assumed to be equal to one. A manager is simply faced with identifying the consequences of available alternatives and selecting the outcome with the highest benefit or payoff.
- Decision-making under risk is when a single action may result in more than one potential outcome, but the relative probability of each outcome is unknown.
- Decisions under conditions of risk are perhaps the most common.
- In such situations, alternatives are recognised, but their resulting consequences are probabilistic and doubtful.
- In practice, managers assess the likelihood of various outcomes occurring based on past experience, research, and other information.
- Decision-making under uncertainty happens when a single action may result in more than one potential outcome, but the relative probability of each outcome is unknown.
- In such situations a manager has no knowledge whatsoever on which to estimate the likely occurrence of various alternatives.
- Decisions under uncertainty generally occur in cases where no historical data are available from which to infer probabilities or in instances which are so novel and complex that it is impossible to make comparative judgements.
- Managers may have to make assumptions from which to forge the decision.

— Managers may have to come up with creative approaches to alternatives and use personal judgment to determine which alternative is best.

— Selection of a new advertising programme is an example of such a decision.

— Decision-making under ambiguity means that the goals to be achieved or the problem to be solved is unclear, alternatives are difficult to define, and information about outcomes is unclear.

— Such problems, referred to as "wicked" decision problems are associated with managerial conflicts over goals and decision alternatives, rapidly changing circumstances, fuzzy information, and unclear linkages among decision elements.

— In such cases managers must conjure up goals and develop reasonable scenarios for decision alternatives in the absence of information.

MODELS OF DECISION-MAKING PROCESS

There are three suggested models of how decisions are made:

— The econological or economic man model.

— The bounded rationality or administrative man model.

— The implicit favourite or gamesman model.

The Econological or Economic Man model represents the earliest attempt to model decision process. This model rests on two assumptions:

1. It assumes that people are economically rational and that they will select the decision or course of action that has the greatest advantage or payoff from among the many alternatives.

2. It also assumes that people attempt to maximise outcomes in an orderly and sequential process by going about the search for the best alternative in a planned, orderly, and logical fashion.

A basic econologic decision model suggests the following orderly steps in the decision process:

1. Discover the symptoms of the problem or difficulty;
2. Determine the goal to be achieved or define the problem to be solved;
3. Develop a criterion against which alternative solutions can be evaluated;
4. Identify all alternative courses of action;
5. Consider the consequences of each alternative as well as the likelihood of the occurrence of each;
6. Choose the best alternative by comparing the consequences of each alternative with the decision criterion; and,
7. Act or implement the decision.

The economic man model represents a useful prescription of how decisions should be made, but it does not adequately portray how decisions are actually made. This model is unrealistic since it makes the following assumptions about human beings:

1. People can have complete information;
2. They can accurately recall any information any time they like;
3. People can manipulate all this information in a series of complex calculations to provide expected values; and,
4. People can rank the consequences in a consistent fashion for the purposes of identifying the preferred alternative.

Simon presented the Bounded Rationality or Administrative Man Model. As the name implies, this model, does not assume individual rationality in the decision-making process. Instead, it assumes that people while they may seek the best solutions usually settle for much less because the decisions they confront typically demand greater information processing capabilities than they possess.

They seek a kind of bounded (or limited) rationality in decisions. The concept of bounded rationality attempt to describe decision processes in terms of three mechanisms:

1. *Sequential attention to alternative solutions:* Instead of identifying all possible solutions and selecting the best, the various alternatives are identified and evaluated one at a time.
2. *Use of heuristics:* Decision makers use heuristics to reduce large problems to manageable proportions so that decisions can be made rapidly. They look for obvious solutions or previous solutions that worked in similar situations.
   — A heuristic is a rule which guides the search for alternatives into areas that have a high probability for yielding satisfactory solutions.
3. *Satisfying:* Whereas the econological model focuses on the decision maker as an optimiser, this model sees her or him as a satisficer.

An alternative is optimal if:

1) There exists a set of criteria that permits an alternative to be compared; and,

2) The alternative in question is preferred, by these criteria, to all other alternatives.

An alternative is satisfactory if:

1) There exists a set of criteria that describes minimally satisfactory alternatives; and,
2) The alternative in question meets or exceeds all these criteria.

The bounded rationality model decision-making process is outlined below:

1. Set the goal to be pursued or define the problem to be solved.
2. Establish an appropriate level of aspiration or criterion level.
3. Employ heuristics to narrow problem space to a single promising alternative.
4. If no feasible alternative is identified *(a)* lower the aspiration level, and *(b)* begin the search for a new alternative solution (repeat steps 2 and 3).
5. After identifying a feasible alternative, evaluate it to determine its acceptability.
6. If the identified alternative is unacceptable, initiate search for a new alternative solution.
7. If the identified alternative is acceptable, implement the solution.
8. Following implementation, evaluate the ease with which the goal was (or was not) attained, and raise or lower level of aspiration accordingly on future decisions of this type.

In contrast to the prescriptive econologic model, it is claimed that the bounded rationality model is descriptive; that is, it describes how decision makers actually arrive at the identification of solutions to organisational problems.

Implicit Favourite or Gamesman Model was developed by Soelberg. In this process, an implicit favourite is identified very early in the choice process during the generation of alternatives.

The search for additional choices is continued and quickly the best alternative candidate is selected, known as the confirmation candidate.

Next, decision rules are generated to demonstrate unequivocally that the implicit favourite is superior to the alternative confirmation candidate.

This is done through perceptual distortion of information about the two alternatives and through weighing systems designed to highlight the positive features of the implicit favourite.

The decision rules are designed to contain only those one or two dimensions in which the implicit favourite can be shown to be superior to the confirmation candidate.

The following are the steps in the process of this model:

1. Set goal;
2. Identify implicit favourite;
3. Compare and rank implicitly rejected alternatives;
4. Identify confirmation candidate;
5. Establish decision rule or criterion;
6. If decision rule does not justify implicit favourite repeat steps 4 and/or 5;
7. Otherwise, announce decision; and,
8. Act.

3

ORGANISATIONAL PLANNING

Planning is the most crucial part of the functions of the manager. The importance of planning cannot be over emphasised. It has been rightly said that failure to plan is planning to fail. Most of the organisations very often fail due to poor planning. In spite of all the resources one may have, without planning one cannot move ahead. Planning is determining the objectives and formulating the methods to achieve them. However, the concept is simpler said than done. It is believed that a job well planned is half done. During planning one need to ask oneself the following:

— What am I trying to accomplish? Or, what is my objective?

— What resources do I have? And what resources do I need to accomplish these objectives?

— What are the methods and means to achieve the objectives?

— Is this the optimal path?

Good and effective managers are positive in their approach and are optimistic. They always prepare themselves for the worst. Though one cannot foresee the future, but one should learn to anticipate. No one can wail till the problems develop before preparing to tackle them. This is called being "proactive." It is, thus, an essential ingredient of planning.

Planning needs choosing the best course of action among many alternatives and decision making. If one is left with no alternatives, there is no scope for planning or choosing. It is essentially an intellectual process requiring knowledge, experience and intelligence. Planning is needed to make things happen or to cope up with the changes. In other circumstances, one can simply be a spectator and watch things in action.

TYPES OF PLANNING

We have seen that planning is essential for the success and survival of any organisation. One should also understand that there exist many different types of plans. One can plan effectively only if one understands the different types of plans and its purposes. Planning involves dealing with the following organisational aspects:

- — Purposes or missions of the organisation
- — Objectives of the organisation
- — Strategies for development
- — Policies for the organisation
- — Procedures as general guidelines
- — Rules for all the departments
- — Programs for action
- — Budgets for monetary purposes

Designing the purpose or the mission is the basic planning activity that all organisations perform. For example, the purpose of the university is teaching and research and that of courts is to interpret laws.

Objective is the ultimate goal toward which the activities of the organisation are directed. In case of a university, teaching, research and enlightening of students are the objectives. The objective of the examination department of a university would be to conduct the exam in a fair and reliable manner and declare the results on time. Though the objectives of the departments are different, they are consistent with the purpose. One department alone is not capable of accomplishing the purpose.

Strategy is the process of determining the major objectives of an organisation and the policies. It is a programme that governs the acquisition, use and disposition of resources to achieve those objectives. In other words, strategy is the general programme of action and deployment of resources to attain comprehensive objectives. Thus, an entrepreneur needs to decide what kind of business he/she is going to do. A strategy may also involve designing a set of policies for the sales department of an organisation. Treatment of strategy as a type of plan is justified by its practical advantage and the importance it is likely to have in giving guidance.

Policy is a general statement or understanding which guides or channel thinking in decision-making. Policy defines an area within which a decision is to be made and ensures that the decision is consistent with the objectives of an organisation. Procedure is a subdivision of policy. It states a series of related steps or tasks to be performed in a sequence. In common parlance it is called standard operating procedure.

Rule is also a plan that prescribes a course of action and explicitly states what is to be done under a given set of circumstances. Here, you need to observe the differences between rules, procedures and policies. The policies are guide to decision-making and allow the managers to use their discretion. Rules and procedures allow no such discretion.

Programme is a rather broad term. It is define as a comprehensive plan that includes future use of different resources in an integrated pattern and establishes a sequence of required actions and time schedules for each in order to achieve the stated objectives. Thus, a programme includes objectives, policies, procedures, methods, standards and budgets. For example, launching of a satellite will require programming.

Budget is a statement of expected results expressed in numerical terms. It is a quantitative expression of a plan. It varies in accuracy, detail and purpose. Master budget contains the consolidated plan of action of the whole enterprise and is in a way the translated version of the overall business plan of the organisation. Production budget is the plan for the production department. The capital expenditure budget, raw, material budget, labour budget etc are budgets for the production department. Some budgets vary according to the organisation's level of output. These are called variable or flexible budgets. Government departments prepare programme budgets in which the agency and the departments identifies goal, develops detailed programs to meet the goals etc. A combination of the variable and the programme budget is zero-based. In this approach, the programmes are started from scratch or zero-base.

PRINCIPLES OF PLANNING

The following principles should be kept in mind while planning effectively:

1. *Take time to plan*—Planning should never be done in haste and repent. One may save some time by developing a plan quickly. But, in the event of things going wrong, if you have not considered all the factors in a hurry, you are under pressure of both the time and resources. This becomes a sure

recipe for trouble. The trouble is not only for the individual, but also for the organisation.

2. *Planning can be top to down or bottom to top*—Generally, the top management of the organisation prepares plans. However, some times the plans evolve from information that comes from the lower levels. This is called bottom to top approach.
3. *Involve and communicate with all those concerned*—Such an exercise inculcates in people a commitment to achieve the goals. Participation in the process of planning gives a sense of pride and binds them to the objectives.
4. *Plans should be flexible and dynamic*—Vision is the art of seeing things that are not apparent. Plans work on similar lines. They should include the factors unexpected or at least should have enough scope for manoeuvring in the event of an unforeseen change in the environment.
5. *Evaluate and revise*—Evaluate the plans at regular intervals to make sure that it is contributing to the objectives in the expected manner.

STEPS IN PLANNING

There is no fixed formula or method for planning. It is carried out as per the need of the organisation. However, one would broadly follow the steps in planning mentioned below:

1. The first step to determine the goals or objectives for the entire organisation. If one fails to set correct or meaningful goals, it becomes impossible to make effective plans. Although goal setting is the first step in planning, the real starting point is the identification of the opportunity or the problem itself. This is very important because the manager

should know where they are, what opportunities or problems they wish to handle and why or what they expect to gain.

2. The second step is to determine the planning premises. Planning premises, in simpler words, is the assumptions that are made about the various elements of the environment. It is important for all the managers involved in planning to agree on the premises. Internal premises include sales forecasts and policies of the organisation. External premises are those factors that are out side the organisation such as technological changes, general economic conditions etc.
3. The third step would be to decide the planning period. While operational planning focus on the short term, the strategic plans focus on the long term.
4. The fourth step in planning is to search for and examine alternative courses of actions. There is rarely a need to plan for where there exist no alternatives and generally an alternative that is not obvious proves to be the best.
5. The fifth step is evaluating the alternatives. After identifying the number of alternatives and examining their strong and weak points, it is logical to evaluate them against the planning premises and objectives.
6. The sixth step is the real point of decision-making. Here, a particular alternative is chosen from the given options. Based on this, the strategic plan is adopted.
7. The seventh step is to make derivative plans. The plan chosen after a through analysis is seldom complete without derivative plans. The plan, to make it operational, is split into departmental plans.

Plans for the various operational units, within the departments, have to be formulated. The plans, thus, developed for the various levels down the organisation are called derivative plans.

After the decisions are made and plans are set and are rolling, in order to reach the desired goal the plan has to be reviewed periodically. Such a review helps in taking corrective action, if necessary, when the plan is in force.

STRATEGIC PLANNING

Nature and Purpose of Strategy

According to the Chinese philosopher Confucius, if the man takes no thought about what is distant, he will find sorrow near at hand. Based on this statement, we interpret that in order to avoid trouble and future adversities one should plan. Strategy, as seen earlier, is the process of determining the major objectives of an organisation. It helps in framing the policies and programs that will govern the acquisition. This will, in turn, help in judiciously using and disposing the resources to achieve those objectives.

Strategic planning is sometimes considered simpler. However, in reality it is not so. It is a highly complicated process that calls for a great degree of analytical skill. It involves analysing the current factors and uncertain future situation external to the organisation and fitting them with its capabilities. To succeed, the strategies should be put into practice. Strategic plans are broken down into smaller plans with great details. Some times the detailed smaller plans, through which the strategies are carried out, are called tactics. A strategy gives the direction to the efforts in which human and material resources will be deployed in order to maximise the chance of achieving the selected goals.

Strategic Planning Process

The following are the steps involved in planning process.

1. Strategies begin with the input available. The input includes the people, capital, technical skills, managerial skill etc.
2. The company profile decides where the company is today and where it should go. Thus, the top managers of the company decide about the business that they should indulge in or the geographical area of operation etc.
3. The overall objectives are targeted toward the entire activities of the company.
4. Both the external and internal environments are to be considered and evaluated.

Companies may also look for alternatives and may diversify, go international or may also think of joint ventures. The various strategies may have to be evaluated before adopting any of them. The vital requirement of a good strategic planning is consistency. There should be uniformity in planning and should also make provision for the unexpected. In other words, one should be prepared for the worst. There should be a contingency plan in place as well. This can prove to be a smart way to plan strategically.

Tools of Strategic Planning

Some following tools help us in the process.

Business Portfolio Matrix

Management thinkers and their associates have over the period of time developed tools to help in planning. Organisations with a relatively high market share and a low growth rate called "cash cows" are well entrenched in the market. Such an organisation provides the cash inflow needed for business activities. The businesses in high market share and enjoying high growth rate are undoubtedly "stars." These give rise to opportunities for growth and profit. Companies with low market share and low growth rate are branded as "dogs." They may be the burden on the other business units and are mostly non-profitable. In all probabilities, they can and generally should be disposed of.

In this case, the business in the quadrant of low market share but has a high growth rate. The question is, what is to be done with them? They really form the question marks. They may move either way. They may move to the left to become the stars or downwards to go to the dogs. However, they may need some financial investment and some time before a decision is made.

The above matrix was developed for organisations with several strategic business units (SBUs). The limitations of the matrix are that the growth rate and the competitive position are inadequate to enable one to take major decisions. Hence, SWOT/TOWS matrix has been introduced for analysing the situation.

SWOT Analysis or TOWS Matrix

This matrix has a wider scope. However, it does not replace the earlier model. It is not sufficient to merely consider the strengths, weakness, opportunities and threats of an organisation. It is important to thoroughly evaluate all of these factors. If you carefully observe the following diagram you will understand the concept better.

	STRENGTHS	WEAKNESS
OPPORTUNITIES	SO	WO
THREATS	ST	WT

Figure 1: The SWOT/TOWS Matrix

The above figure provides four alternative strategies. You should also remember that both the internal and external environments have to be kept in mind while considering the model. The four strategies are as follows:

1. The "SO" strategy is the most preferred one. In this strategy, the organisation can use its strengths and take advantage of the opportunities available to it. All the organisations would try to reach this state of business.
2. In the "ST" strategy, the threats are taken care of with the strengths of the organisation.
3. The "WO" strategy tries to minimise the weaknesses and maximise the opportunities.
4. The "WT" strategy attempts to minimise both the weakness and the threats. In this process, the organisation may try to form a joint venture, reduce or even close down the operation.

The core purpose of the business is to produce products or services. The determination of this purpose decides what the organisation or the business wants to do. There are two basic functions of any business, that are as follows:

— Innovation

— Marketing

A business can scarcely survive without at least one of these functions and preferably both. Marketing strategies are designed to guide managers to elicit a behavioural response from the customers. There are three generic strategies. These prove as a good starting point for strategic thinking. They are as follows:

— Overall cost leadership

— Differentiation

— Focus

In overall cost leadership the idea is to reduce expenditure within the enterprise. Cost reduction helps in gaining a large market share. "Nirma" is a leading practitioner of this strategy. The limitation of this strategy is that others may also follow suit and may shake the very foundation of the organisation. In differentiation, the company tries to achieve superior performance or offer something unique and seeks a leadership status. A good example is Intel. It established itself as a technology leader by introducing new microprocessors at breakneck speed. In focus strategy, the company focuses on one or more narrow market segments or special groups of customers. Instead of serving the total industry with its products or services, the company may choose a specific segment of the market. The company can follow the low cost strategy or differentiation or both. Once the strategy planning has been done, it should work out the detailed supporting programmes to be effective. However, a good strategy cannot meet success without proper implementation. In fact, Copernicus—a leading marketing research and consulting firm—has found that many failures of the strategies are due to poor implementation.

Let us now examine the reasons why strategic planning may fail and also see what can be done to prevent this.

A recent study in management indicated the following reasons for failure of planning:

— Managers are inadequately prepared for strategic planning.

— The premises or the information for preparing the plans is insufficient for planning for action.

— The objectives of the organisation are too vague.

— The SBU's are not clearly defined.

- — The lack of control on the SBU's. In other words, there is insufficient review of strategic plans.
- — The link between planning and control is insufficient.

The following steps can be taken to prevent these failures from happening:

- — Communicating strategies to all key decision-making managers.
- — Ensuring that the action plans contribute to and reflect major objectives and strategies.
- — Reviewing strategies regularly.
- — Developing contingency strategies.
- — Making the organisation structure fit planning needs.
- — Continuing to emphasise planning and implementing strategy.
- — Creating a company climate that forces planning.

4

ORGANISATIONAL DESIGN

An organisational design unambiguously states as to who is to do what and who is responsible for what results. Further, the design should also motivate the performance of the group by removing uncertainty and confusion. It should promote teamwork and facilitate unhindered communication both horizontally and vertically and enable decision-making a smooth process.

ELEMENTS OF ORGANISATIONAL DESIGN

The following are the six key elements of organisational design:

- Stating the organisational objectives.
- Designing the supportive programmes and plans.
- Identifying and classifying the relevant jobs necessary to achieve the organisational objectives.
- Clubbing these jobs and the best way to do them in view of the available resources.
- Placing a manager at the head of the group with the necessary authority.
- Establishing proper control relationship and communication channels within the group and among the other groups.

Here, one needs to keep in mind that there is no fixed or the best way to design an organisation. If there were one, there would have been no need for us to study these theories and so on. It would have been suffice to know the best one and go on.

ORGANISATIONAL STRUCTURE AND ITS DIMENSIONS

Organising means developing intentionally a structure of roles for effective performance of the enterprise. For efficient working of the enterprise, the structure must be clearly understood and principles must be put into practice. Urwick said in his classic book that lack of design in organisation is illogical, cruel, wasteful and inefficient. It is illogical because good design or planning should come first whether one speaks of engineering or social practice. It is cruel because the main sufferers from a lack of design in organisation are those individuals who work in that undertaking. It is wasteful because unless jobs are clearly put together along lines of functional specialisation it is impossible to train new men or women to succeed to positions as the incumbents are promoted, resign or retire. And it is inefficient because if management is not based on principles, it can be said that it is based on personalities with the resultant rise of company politics for a machine will not run smoothly when fundamental engineering principles have been ignored in construction.

Though the principles of organisation have general application, every organisation should identify its own needs before applying them. The organisation's structure should be designed as per its need. The characteristic of an effective organisation is its capability to meet the different needs and make changes as and when required. One prime condition in organising is flexibility. Another point to be kept in mind while organising is organising around people i.e. the available personnel in the organisation should not be thrown away. The structure should be modified to fit a person as per his/her capabilities.

Need for Reorganisation

Keeping in view the changes occurring in the environment that are both internal and external, one may need to reorganise. Another reason could be the proven weakness in the existing enterprise. Even the personality clashes between the managers also may be solved by reorganisation.

Making the Organisation Work

The biggest problem in the organisation is the misunderstanding of the line and staff functions. One way of understanding them is that line functions are those that have direct impact on the achievement of the goals. The staff functions are those that help the line to perform effectively. This concept is the very source of problem. As per the above, production, sales and finance are line functions and purchasing, HR, maintenance, quality control and security are staff functions. Here, one wonders if it is correct that failure to pass the quality test shall bring the production and sales to a grinding halt? Then, how should the line and staff be defined? It is good to keep in mind that they are simply a matter of relationships. Let us look at the scalar principle in organisation. The clearer the line of authority from the ultimate management position in an enterprise to every subordinate position, the clearer will be the responsibility for decision making and the more effective will be organisation communication. It is now clear from the above principle that line relationship is in which a superior exercises direct control over the subordinate where as staff relationship is advisory.

Authority and Power

You should clearly understand the difference between authority and power. Authority is the right to decision-making that can affect others. In an organisation it stems from the position in the structure. Power is the ability of the person to influence the other person. A person can get power from different sources. Legitimate power is derived from the position one holds in the organisation. One may get power from the knowledge–such as lawyers, doctors and teachers to name a few. Referent power is the one acquired due to one's personality or the influence one has over the others–like Mahatma Gandhi or say Nelson Mandela for example. Power also arises out the ability to grant rewards to other; thus reward power is the power to grant or withhold something. For example the teachers or professors have considerable reward power since they can grant or refuse grades. In contrast, there exist power to punish too. This type of power is known as coercive power.

Functional authority is a small piece of line authority. It is the right delegated to an individual or a department to control specified processes or other matters relating to activities undertaken by persons in other departments. For example, the Managing Director has overall authority on the enterprise and is limited only by the superior authority as the Board of Directors and Government regulations. The people of personnel, accounting, purchasing or public relations have no part of this line authority. Now if the MD delegates to these staff the right to issue instructions directly, the right is called functional authority. This functional authority has to be carefully used. A purchasing manager's functional authority is limited to setting the procedures for purchasing and does not include telling departments what they can purchase or when.

The importance of staff functions should not be underestimated. In the present environment, the line managers cannot do without specialists' knowledge. However the advisory departments only forwards a plan and it is for the others to take the decision and execute it – an ideal situation for shifting blame for failures. Great care should be taken to avoid such mishaps. Good managers should posses the analytical power and identify the weaknesses and correct them at the acceptance stage itself. Too much of staff interference will complicate line control. Although some multiple commands may be unavoidable due to functional authority, managers should remain aware of these keep it well under control.

Decentralisation

Decentralisation is the process of assigning the decision-making authority in an enterprise. There could not be absolute centralisation or decentralisation. In both the cases, it means there are no managers and no organisational structure. But this is not the case always. Hence, some decentralisation exists in all business houses. But, how much should be delegated? Without delegation, even the best of managers cannot improve the organisation's performance unless they can use their discretion or exploit the knowledge one has. Studies have shown that the managers and the organisations fail mainly due to poor delegation of authority.

Art of Delegation

As stated above failures occur mainly due to poor delegation and it is not due to managers are not aware about delegation but because they are not willing to apply them. This is largely due to personal attitudes. Therefore, the following points would help in effective delegation:

1. Nominate a person and delegate in line with the results expected. This includes assigning enough authority to do the job effectively and achieve the stated objective.
2. Maintain proper control and good communication. By control, we do not mean interfering in the actions of the subordinate but to observe and take corrective actions on deviations from the plans.

Advantages of decentralisation

— Relives top management of some burden of decision-making and forces upper level managers to let go.

— Encourages decision-making and assumption of authority and responsibility.

— Gives managers more freedom and independence in decision-making.

— Promotes establishment and use of broad controls which may increase motivation.

— Makes comparison of performance of different organisational units.

— Helps in setting up profit centres.

— Facilitates product diversification

— Promotes development of general managers.

— Aids in adaptation to fast-changing environment.

Limitations of decentralisation

— Makes it more difficult to have a uniform policy.

— Increases complexity of coordination of decentralised organisational units.

— May result in loss of some control by upper-level managers.

— May be limited by inadequate control techniques.

— May be constrained by inadequate planning and control systems.

— Can be limited by the availability of qualified managers.

— Involves considerable expenses for training managers.

— May be limited by external forces (national labour unions, governmental controls, tax policies).

— May not be favoured by economies of scale of some operations.

ADVANTAGES AND DISADVANTAGES OF ORGANISATIONAL DESIGN

Before we proceed to look into the different types of organisational designs it would do good to understand the formal and the informal organisational set up that exists in any given enterprise.

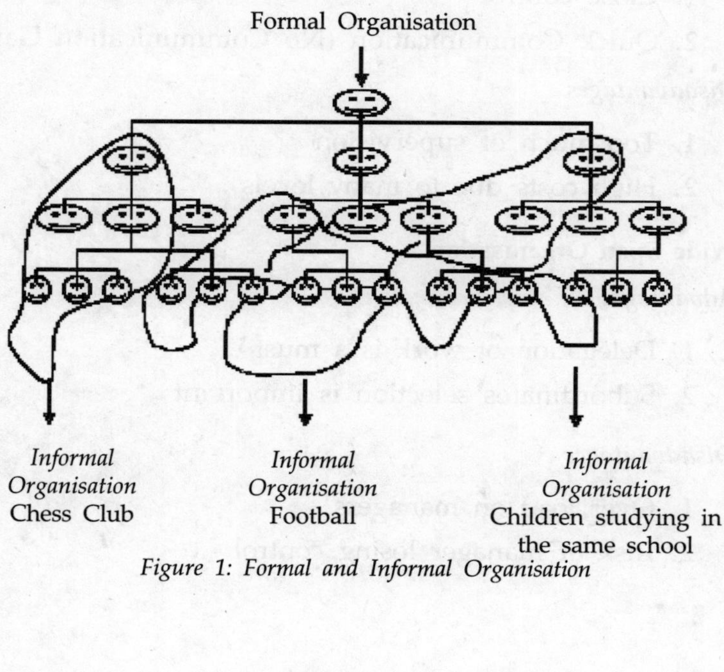

Figure 1: Formal and Informal Organisation

From the figure 1 it would be clear as to what is meant by formal and informal organisation. By formal organisation we mean the structure created intentionally. Whenever a formal organisation is created, generally an informal organisation also comes into being. An informal organisation can be defined as a network of personal and social relations not established or required by the formal organisation but arising spontaneously as people associate with one another. Thus informal organisation might include the people who play chess, whose children study in the same school etc.

The process of organising is departmentalisation. By department we mean a distinct area, division or branch of an enterprise for the performance of specified job over which a manager has control and authority.

Narrow Span Organisation

Advantages

1. Close control
2. Quick Communication (No Communication Gap)

Disadvantages

1. Too much of supervision
2. High costs due to many levels

Wide Span Organisation

Advantages

1. Delegation of work is a must
2. Subordinates selection is important

Disadvantages

1. Over load on managers
2. Risk of manager losing control

(*a*) The levels are expensive.

(*b*) The levels complicate communication.

(*c*) The levels also complicate planning and control.

The principle of the span of management states that there is a limit to the number of subordinates a manager can effectively supervise, but the exact number will depend on the impact of underlying factors.

Personal intelligence and factors such as comprehending, good interpersonal skills, communication abilities and leadership qualities influence the size of the span. If it were that the size of the span of control is limited then the size of the enterprise is also limited. But that is not so. This is because of the recourse of departments. In theory, by creating departments an organisation can expand to any size.

Departmentalisation by Numbers

As the name implies, this process is simply departmentalisation by the numbers. Though this was an important method earlier it is now losing its value. Its advantage is its simplicity. The following are its disadvantages:

- The need for specialised and various skills
- Lack of efficiency
- Its lack of usefulness at higher level

Departmentalisation by Time

Certain businesses cannot be stopped or started at short intervals or it is not viable or it cannot be done so. For example, running of trains and hospital needs round the clock working compelling work to be carried out in three shifts. Thus comes the departmentalisation by time. Its advantages are as follows:

1. Services can be provided round the clock or at least beyond the 8-hour shift.
2. Better use of the machines–using the same machine for more than 8 hours.
3. People can work at different time of the day and hence can take advantage of the rest of the day–like the students can work in the evening shifts etc.
4. Processes requiring more than 8 hours at a stretch can also be undertaken.

Its disadvantages are as follows:

1. Coordination and communication will be major problem–though it can be tackled one need to take great care as there are chances for lapses.
2. Supervision during the night shifts is generally lax.
3. There is always a fatigue factor setting in either in men or in machine.

Departmentalisation by Function

Departmentalisation by function is the most common basis for organising. Marketing, Production and Administration are widely used departments. Its advantages are as follows:

1. It is an established method.
2. It allows specialisation on the part of the managers.
3. The top managers are able to defend the activities of the enterprise and have close control over the affairs.

Its disadvantages are as follows:

1. The persons working in the respective departments have difficulty in seeing the business as a whole.
2. This kind of departmentalisation makes it difficult to adapt quickly to environmental changes.

Departmentalisation by Area

Departmentalisation by geographical area is also a very common approach. This kind of approach is useful to large-scale operations and operations carried over large geographical area. Area wise departmentalisation is most often used in sales and in production where as finance is usually located at the corporate office. Its advantages are as follows:

1. Local market's needs and problems can be handled.
2. Since the manager in a territory has to carry out many different functional and managerial activities, this type of organisation provides a good training ground for general managers.

Its disadvantages are as follows:

1. Instead of specialists this approach requires more persons with general managerial abilities.
2. It may increase the problem of control by the top management.

Departmentalisation by Product

Grouping activities on the basis of product or product lines has long been growing in importance in multi-line and large-scale enterprises. Its advantages are as follows:

1. It permits the maximum use of personal skills and specialised knowledge.
2. Profit responsibility can be exacted from product department managers.

Its disadvantages are as follows:

1. Similar to the area departmentalisation, it is important to have people with general abilities.
2. Problem of maintaining top management control.

Matrix Organisation

Other names given to this type of organisation are Grid or Project or Product management. The essence of matrix organisation normally is the combining of functional and product patterns of departmentalisation in the same organisation structure. There are functional managers in charge of engineering functions and an overlay of project managers responsible for the end product. Though this kind of organisation is followed in many businesses it may not be drawn as a matrix explicitly.

Its advantages are as follows:

1. Professional identification is possible.
2. Product profitability can be easily identified.

Its disadvantages are as follows:

1. Loss of unity of command.
2. Conflicts in authority exist and so managers with highly skillful interpersonal relations are required.

Strategic Business Units

SBUs are distinct businesses with its own mission that is distinct from the other units. It has its own manager, competitors, plans and resource management.

Its advantages are as follows:

1. It preserves the attention and energies of a manager and staff to guide and promote a product etc.
2. It promotes entrepreneurship.

Its disadvantages are as follows:

1. In practice, it is difficult to design
2. It is difficult to define SBU.

5

ORGANISATIONAL LEADERSHIP

The management of an organisation is responsible for putting this human resource into effective use. Management can get the results from people in an organisation in the following two ways:

- By exercise authority vested in it
- By winning support of the people

Thus, leadership is an essential ingredient for successful organisations. A successful organisation has one major attribute that sets it apart from unsuccessful organisation. This aspect is dynamic and effective leadership. Leadership is the process of influencing the behaviour of others to work willingly and enthusiastically for achieving predetermined goals. Any type of compliance, tending towards resistance, is unwillingly. On the other hand, compliance tending towards commitment is willingly and enthusiastically. The latter type of response is the objective of leadership:

> "Leadership is interpersonal influence exercised in a situation and directed through communication process, towards the attainment of a specified goal or goals."
>
> —*Tennenbaum*

This definition puts emphasis on influencing through communication. However, it does not emphasize the enthusiasm with which the receiver of the communication will act. Other definition is as follows:

> "Leadership is essentially a continuous process of influencing behaviour. A leader breathes life into the group and motivates it towards goals. The lukewarm desires for achievement are transformed into a burning passion for accomplishment."

A more recent definition of leadership is as follows:

> "Leadership is the process of influencing and supporting others to work enthusiastically toward achieving objectives."

An analysis of these definitions brings out certain specific features of leadership. They are as follows:

1. Leadership is a continuous process of behaviour. It is not a one-shot activity
2. Leadership may be seen in terms of relationship between a leader and his/her followers. This can include an individuals or a group. This relationship arises out of their functioning for common goals.
3. By exercising leadership, the leader tries to influence the behaviour of individuals or group of individuals. This influenced behaviour helps in achieving the common goals.
4. The followers work willingly and enthusiastically to achieve the goals. Thus, there is no coercive force which induces the followers to work.
5. Leadership helps the followers in attaining common goals. It happens when the leader feels the importance of individuals, gives them recognition and conveys them about the importance of activities performed by them.
6. Leadership is exercised in a particular situation, at a given point of time. This is under specific circumstances. It implies that leadership styles maybe different under different situations.

DIFFERENCE BETWEEN LEADERSHIP AND MANAGEMENT

The above definitions and characteristics of leadership indicate that leadership and management are related but they are not the same. A person can be an effective manager, a leader, both or neither. This is due to the fact that leadership differs from management on some counts. The leadership differs from management in terms of the emphasis that is put on the following four activities:

1. Creating an agenda.
2. Developing a human network for achieving the agenda.
3. Executing plans.
4. Outcomes of activities.

While leadership emphasizes change in these activities, management believes in status quo. Stephen Covey, a consultant on developing leadership, has emphasized the difference between leadership and management as follows:

1. Leadership deals with vision after keeping the mission in sight. It also deals with effectiveness and results. Management deals with establishing structure and systems to get the results. It focuses on efficiency, cost-benefit analysis, logistics, methods, procedures and policies.
2. Leadership focuses on top line management. The management, on the other hand, focuses on the lower level workers. Leadership derives its power from values and correct principles. Management organises resources to serve selected objectives to produce the bottom line.
3. Leadership inspires and motivates people to work together with a common vision and purpose. Management involves controlling and monitoring

results against plans, identifying deviations and then planning and organising to solve the problems.

4. Leadership emphasizes transformation aspect and, therefore, transformational leadership emerges. Management focuses on transactional aspect. This leads to the emergence of transactional leadership. Transformational leadership involves a set of abilities that allows leaders to recognise the need for change, to create a vision to guide that change and to execute that change effectively. Transactional leadership involves routine, regimented activities-assigning work, evaluating performance, making decisions and other related activities.

Based on the above discussion, the differences between leadership and management are summarised in the following Table 1.

Table 1: Difference between leadership and management

Factors	*Leadership*	*Management*
1. Source of power	Personal abilities	Authority delegated
2. Focus	Vision and purpose	Operating results
3. Approach	Transformational	Transactional
4. Process	Inspiration	Control
5. Emphasis	Collectivity	Individualism
6. Futurity	Proactive	Reactive
7. Type	Formal and informal	Formal

Informal and Formal Leaders

Leaders arise in many situations. Even informal social groups have leaders. When groups endure and become formal, the persons are elected as leaders. Normally, the persons elected to offices are the ones who are the natural leaders of the groups. Their views get attention from other members even without formal election, but with election, those natural leaders are consciously acknowledged. Researches based on small groups show that those persons who emerge as informal leaders are perceived by other group members as being the best able to satisfy the group needs. These leaders, therefore, are enabled to influence other members. A leader derives his/her influence from member's feelings or intuitions. This helps the person in satisfying their needs. Consequently, they are willing to submit, within the limits, to the leader's guidance.

When a person, either an informal leader or someone else, is appointed in a superior capacity, the natural leadership relations change. Such change occurs in two respects. First, when a person is appointed in superior capacity, he/she gets authority from the organisation. This authority enables the individual to increase or decrease the satisfaction of one's subordinates. Second, because of appointment, the person has the obligation of achieving organisational objectives besides an obligation to provide satisfaction to one's subordinates. An appointed or formal leader cannot solely rely upon the use of authority for getting desired results from the subordinates. This is because the subordinates seldom put maximum effort under the pressure of authority. Thus, a chief executive having more authority, but lacking leadership qualities, may be less effective as compared to a foreman with less authority but high degree of leadership qualities. Regardless of these differences between formal and informal leaders, however, a leader is able to direct the actions of the followers because they believe the person can provide rewards or prevent penalties. This satisfies their needs.

IMPORTANCE OF LEADERSHIP

Leadership is an important factor that adds to the success of any organisation. Throughout history, the importance of leadership has been recognised. The difference between success and failure in a war, a political movement, a business or a team game can be attributed largely to leadership.

Without a good leader, organisation cannot function efficiently and effectively. Since the organisation is basically a deliberate creation of human beings for certain specified objectives, the activities of its members need to be directed in a certain way. Any departure from this way can lead to inefficiency in the organisation. The leader affects direction of activities in the organisation. The importance of good leadership can be discussed as follows:

1. *Motivating employees*—Motivation is necessary for work performance. When the motivation level is high, the performance is better. A good leader, by exercising efficient leadership, motivates the employees for high performance. Good leadership in the organisation itself is a motivating factor for workers.
2. *Creating confidence*—A good leader can create confidence in one's followers by directing them, giving them advice and inducing good results through them in the organisation. An individual, with the help of a leader, can work with high efficiency. The employee tries to maintain this efficiency level as one acquires certain level of confidence toward one's capacity. Sometimes, individuals fail to recognise their qualities and capabilities to work in the absence of good direction.

3. *Building morale*—Morale is expressed as attitudes of employees toward the organisation, the management and voluntary cooperation to offer their ability to the organisation. High morale leads to high productivity and organisational stability.

By providing good leadership in the organisation, employee's morale can be raised. This ensures that high productivity and stability is maintained in the organisation. Thus, good leadership is essential in all aspects of managerial functions whether it be motivation, communication or direction. Good leadership ensures success in the organisation. On the other hand, unsatisfactory human performance in any organisation can be primarily attributed to poor leadership.

Leadership has probably been written about, formally researched and informally discussed more than any other single topic in the field of management. Despite all the attention given to it, leadership still remains as being a "black box" or unexplainable phenomenon. It is known to exist and to have tremendous influence on human performance. However, its inner workings and specific dimensions cannot be precisely spelled out.

Many of the research studies, particularly by behavioural scientists, have been carried on to find out the answer of the following question:

— What makes a leader effective?

— Is a leader's success attributable to the person's personality, behaviour or the types of followers one has?

— Can success be situation related or is it a result of combination of all the above factors?

These researchers, however, could not give a satisfactory answer of the question. Instead, their researches have resulted in various theories or approaches on leadership. The prominent amongst these are the following:

— Trait theory
— Behavioural theory
— Situational theory

Age-old theories of leadership, known as great man theory or charismatic leadership theory, have been discarded long back by behavioural scientists. They have started attracting attention recently. Each of these theories has its own contributions, limitations, assumptions and framework of analysis.

Charismatic Leadership Theory

Charismatic leadership theory, also called great man theory, can be traced back to ancient times. Plato's *Republic* and Confucius' *Analects* dealt with leadership. They provided some insights into the leadership theory. Subsequent studies based on these insights have suggested that a leader is born and is not made. A leader has some charisma which acts as influencer. Charisma is a Greek word which means gift. Thus, charisma is a God-gifted attribute in a person which makes a person a leader irrespective of the situations in which the person works. Charismatic leaders are those who inspire followers and have a major impact on their organisations through their personal vision and energy. Occasionally, a leader emerges whose high visibility and personal charisma catches the public consciousness.

Robert House, who proposed a re-look on charismatic theory, suggests that charismatic leaders have very high levels of referent power and that some of that power comes from their need to influence others. According to him, a charismatic leader has extremely high levels of self-confidence, dominance and a strong conviction in the normal righteousness of his/her beliefs. It has the ability to convince the followers that he/she possesses such confidence and conviction. He suggests further that charismatic leaders communicate a vision or higher-level goal that captures the commitment and energy of followers. The basic assumptions and implications of charismatic leadership theory are as follows:

1. Leaders in general, and great leaders in particular, have some exceptional inborn leadership qualities which are bestowed upon them by the divine power.
2. These inborn qualities are sufficient for a leader to be successful.
3. Since these qualities are inborn, these cannot be enhanced through education and training. Further, since these qualities are of personal nature, others cannot share these.
4. These leadership qualities make a leader effective and situational factors do not have any influence.

Implications of the Theory

Charismatic leadership theory has re-emerged basically for two reasons. First, many large companies in USA have embarked on organisational transformation programmes of extensive changes that should be accomplished within a short period of time. It is believed that such transformations require transformational leaders. Second, many feel that by concentrating on traits, behaviours and situations, leadership theories have lost sight of the leaders. These theories discuss more about transactional leaders and not about transformational leaders. A transactional leader determines what subordinates need to do to achieve objectives, classifies those requirements and helps subordinates become confident that they can reach their objectives. A transformational leader inspires his/her followers through vision and energy. Trait, behavioural, and situational leadership theories fail to explain the reasons behind the deeds of great political leaders like Mahatma Gandhi, Lenin, etc. These leaders have been known for transforming their nations. In India, Great industrialists like JRD Tata, GD Birla and Dhirubhai Ambani have created vast industrial empires because of their vision, energy and entrepreneurship. Charismatic leadership theory focuses on such qualities.

It is important to mention here that there are two basic limitations of this theory. Firstly, if we assume that there are certain inborn qualities of a great leader, it implies that nothing can be done to develop leaders in an organisation. In fact, its opposite is also true. Through various training and development programmes, leaders, can be developed in an organisation. Secondly, a charismatic leader may fail in the changed situation. For example, Winston Churchill, the late prime minister of Great Britain, was very effective during Word War II. He, however, flopped afterwards. Thus, we can derive that the situational variables play their own role in determining leadership effectiveness.

Trait Theory

The weaknesses of charismatic leadership theory gave way to a more realistic approach to leadership. Under the influence of the behaviourist psychological thought, researchers accepted the fact that leadership traits are not completely inborn but can also be acquired through learning and experience. Trait is defined as relatively enduring quality of an individual. The trait approach seeks to determine what makes a successful leader from the leaders own personal characteristics. From the very beginning, people have emphasized that a particular individual was a successful leader because of certain qualities or characteristics. Trait approach leadership studies were quite popular between 1930 and 1950. The method of study was to select leaders of eminence and their characteristics were studied. It was believed that only people with certain specific traits could become successful leaders.

Various research studies suggest that intelligence, attitude, personality and biological factors are essential ingredients for effective leaders. Various trait theories suggest the following traits of a successful leader:

— Physical and constitutional factor such as height, weight, physique, energy, health, appearance

— Intelligence

— Self-confidence

— Sociability

— Will, initiative, persistence, ambition

— Dominance

— Other factors such as ability to talk, cheerfulness, geniality, enthusiasm, perseverance, alertness and originality

In a later study, researchers found supervisory ability, achievement motivation, self-actualisation, intelligence, self-assurance and decisiveness as the qualities related with leadership success.

The current research on leadership traits suggests that some factors do help differentiate leaders from non-leaders. These traits are as follows:

— High level personal drive

— Desire to lead

— Personal integrity

— Self-confidence

Cognitive or analytical ability, business knowledge, charisma, creativity, flexibility and personal warmth are also frequently desired. Anderson Consulting, a management consultancy firm, conducted a study of 90 global chief executives to find out the abilities required for an ideal chief executive in the present era of globalisation. The study highlighted 14 qualities. Accordingly, a chief executive thinks globally, anticipates opportunity, creates a shared vision, develops and empowers people, appreciates cultural diversity, builds teamwork and partnership, embraces change, is technologically savvy, encourages constructive challenge, ensures customer satisfaction, achieves a competitive advantage, demonstrates personal mastery, shares leadership, and lives the values. Various studies show wide variation in leadership traits. Based on their source, traits can be classified as innate and acquirable traits.

An individual possesses innate qualities since birth. These qualities are natural and often known as God-gifted. On the basis of the 11 qualities, it is said that leaders are born and not made. Individuals cannot acquire these qualities. The following are some of the innate qualities that a successful leader has:

1. *Physical features*—Physical features of a man are determined by heredity factors. Heredity is the transmission of the qualities from ancestor to descendant through a mechanism lying primarily in the chromosomes of the germ cells. Physical characteristics and rate of maturation determine the personality formation which is important factor in determining leadership success. To some extent, height, weight, physique, health and appearance are important for leadership.

2. *Intelligence*—For leadership, higher level of intelligence is required. Intelligence is generally expressed in terms of mental ability. Intelligence, to a very great extent, is a natural quality in the individuals because it is directly related with brain. The composition of brain is a natural factor.

However, many psychologists claim that the level of intelligence in an individual can be increased through various training methods.

Acquirable qualities of leadership are those which can be acquired and increased through various processes. In fact, when a child is born, he/she learns many behavioural patterns through socialisation and identification processes. Such behavioural patterns develop in a child over a period time. Many of these traits can be increased through training programmes. The following are certain major qualities that are essential for leadership:

1. *Emotional stability*—A leader should have high level of emotional stability. The person should be free from bias, consistent in action and refrain oneself from anger. It is important to be well adjusted and staying away from anti-social attitudes. Self-confidence and the ability to face all situations are important traits in this respect.
2. *Human relations*—A successful leader should have adequate knowledge of human relations. Since an important part of a leader's job is to develop people and get their voluntary cooperation for achieving work, a leader should have intimate knowledge of people and relationships within each group. The knowledge of how human beings behave and how they react to various situations is quite meaningful to a leader.
3. *Empathy*—Empathy relates to observing the things or situations from others' points of view. The ability to look at things objectively and understanding them from others' point of view is an important aspect of successful leadership. When one is empathetic, the person is aware of what makes the other fellows think as they do.

4. *Objectivity*—Objectivity implies that what a leader does should be based on relevant facts and information. He should assess these without any bias or prejudice. The leader must base his relationship on his objectivity. He is objective and does not permit himself to get emotionally involved to the extent that he finds it difficult to make an objective diagnosis and implement the action required.
5. *Motivating skills*—Not only a leader is self-motivated, but the person also has the requisite quality to motivate his/her followers. Though there are many external forces which motivate a person for higher performance, there is inner drive in people also for motivation to work. The leader can play active role in stimulating these inner drives of the followers. Thus, a leader should understand people to the extent that the person knows his/her ability to activate others.
6. *Technical skills*—Leading a group requires adherence to definite principles which should be understood and followed for greater success. The ability to plan, organise, delegate, analyse, seek advice, make decision, control and win cooperation requires the use of important abilities which constitute technical competence of leadership. The technical competence of leader may win support from the followers.
7. *Communicative skills*—A successful leader knows how to communicate effectively. Communication has great force in getting the acceptance from the receivers of communication. A leader uses communication skilfully for persuasive, informative, and stimulating purposes. Normally, a successful leader is extrovert.

8. *Social skills*—A successful leader has social skills. The leader understands people and knows their strengths and weaknesses. He/she has the ability to work with people and conducts oneself with confidence and loyalty. This helps in getting cooperation from people willingly.

Though all these qualities contribute to the success of leadership, the same cannot be applied to the relative contributions of these qualities. Moreover, it is not necessary that a successful leader in equal quantity possess all these qualities. The list of qualities may be only suggestive and not comprehensive. Leadership is too nebulous a concept to be definitely identified by listing of its important attributes.

Implications of the Theory

This theory has two very important implications. Firstly, the theory indicates that a leader requires some traits and qualities to be effective. Secondly, many of these qualities may be developed in individuals through training and development programs. However, the theory suffers from two sets of limitations. These are as follows:

- Generalisation of traits
- Applicability of traits

Generalisation of traits—There are problems in identifying traits which may be relevant for a leader to be effective in all situations. For example, Jennings has concluded that, fifty years of study has failed to produce a one-personality trait or set of qualities that can be used to discriminate leaders and non-leaders. The various studies on traits have failed to uncover any traits that clearly and consistently distinguish leaders and followers. Many other behavioural scientists hold similar views. From this point of view, the theory suffers from the following limitations:

1. There cannot be generalisation of traits for a successful leader. This is evident through various researches conducted on leadership traits.
2. No evidence has been given about the degree of the various traits because people have various traits with different degrees.
3. There is a problem of measuring the traits. Though there are various tests to measure the personality traits, no definite conclusion can be drawn.

Applicability of traits—There is another set of problems that hinder full application of trait theory in practice. Leadership, as a process of influence, reflects in a leader's behaviour and not in personal traits. There have been professionals with leadership traits who failed to become effective leaders. The reason for this phenomenon is that there is no direct cause-effect relationship between a trait of a person and his/her behaviour. The trait may be only one of the factors shaping behaviour. The other factors, sometimes even more important, are situational variables. These situational variables are not incorporated in the trait theory.

Behavioural Theory

Behavioural theory of leadership emphasizes on strong leadership qualities. These qualities are direct results of effective role behaviour. Leadership is shown by a person's acts more than by his/her traits. Researchers exploring leadership role have come to the conclusion that to operate effectively, groups need someone to perform the following two functions:

— Task-related functions

— Group maintenance functions

Task-related functions, or problem solving functions, together provide solutions to the problems faced by the groups in performing jobs and activities. Group maintenance functions, or social functions, relate to actions of mediating disputes and ensuring that individuals feel valued by the group. An individual, who is able to perform both roles successfully, would be an effective leader. These two roles may require two different sets of behaviour from the leader, known as leadership styles.

Leadership behaviour may be viewed in the following two ways:

— Functional

— Dysfunctional

Functional behaviour influences followers positively and includes functions such as setting clear goals, motivating employees for achieving goals, raising their level of morale, building team spirit, effective two-way communication etc. Dysfunctional behaviour is unfavourable for the followers and denotes ineffective leadership. Such a behaviour may reflect inability to accept work force's ideas, display emotional immaturity, poor human relations etc.

Implications of the Theory

Behavioural theory of leadership has some important implications for managers. They can shape their behaviour which appears functional and discard the behaviour which appears dysfunctional. Researchers used the behavioural theory for analysing leadership behaviour, also known as leadership styles. They have prescribed various leadership styles which may be applied while managing people in organisations. This theory suffers from two basic limitations.

First, a particular behaviour may be functional at a point of time but it may be dysfunctional at another point of time. Thus, the time element is a decider of the effectiveness of a particular behaviour and not the behaviour itself. Second, effectiveness of leadership behaviour depends on various factors that are not innately present in a leader. These factors are external to the leader like nature of followers or subordinates and the situations under which the leader's behaviour takes place. These factors have not been given adequate consideration. To that extent, the theory does not explain leadership phenomenon fully.

Situational Theory

Situational leadership approach was applied for the first time in 1920 in the armed forces of Germany. The objective was to get good generals under different situations. In the business organisations, much emphasis on the leadership researches was placed on the situations that surrounded the exercise of leadership since early 1950s. The prime attention in situational theory of leadership, also known as contingency theory, is given to the situation in which leadership is exercised. Therefore, effectiveness of leadership is affected by factors that are associated with the leader and factors associated with the situation.

The factors that affect effectiveness of leadership can broadly be classified into the following categories:

- Leader's behaviour
- Situational factors

The combination of both these factors determines effectiveness of leadership.

Leader's Behaviour

Leader's behaviour is affected by two variables—leader's characteristics and the hierarchical position that a person has in the organisation.

1. *Leader's characteristics*—An individual's behaviour is influenced by intelligence and ability. It is also influenced by characteristics such as personality, attitudes, interest, motivation and physical characteristics such as age, sex and physical features. The behaviour of a leader is influenced by all these factors. These factors are internal to a leader.
2. *Leader's hierarchical position*—Leader's hierarchical position in the organisation is important because people at different levels face different kind of problems. These affect the degree of participation from superior and subordinates. This degree of participation helps in arriving at decisions which later solve organisational problems. Managers at higher levels are more concerned with long-run complex problems which require more participation in decision-making. Managers at lower levels are more concerned with short-run problems involving the daily operations which may not require high level of participation. The degree of this participation affects the leader's behaviour.

Situational Factors

Besides the leader's related factors, leadership effectiveness is affected by situational factors. These factors affect a leader's behaviour. If a leader matches the requirement of these factors, his/her leadership will be effective. The various situational factors may be grouped into the following four categories:

— Subordinate's characteristics

— Leader's situation

— Group factors

— Organisational factors

1. *Subordinate's characteristics*—Various factors which affect an individual's behaviour, as discussed in the case of a leader, are relevant for the subordinate too.
2. *Leader's situation*—The leader's situation, with respect to his/her subordinates, is an important factor affecting leadership effectiveness. There are two main variables which determine the leader's situation. These are as follows:
   - Leader's position power
   - Leader-subordinate relations

   Leader's position power helps or hinders in influencing others. Thus, high-position power simplifies the leader's task of influencing others, while low-position power makes the leader's task more difficult. Another factor is leader subordinate relation. It is based on the classic exchange theory which suggests that there is a two-way influence in social relationships. Thus, good followers need to succeed in their own jobs with the help of the leader while helping their leaders to succeed at theirs. Thus, if the leader has good subordinates and good relations with them, he/she is likely to be more effective.
3. *Group factors*—Various group factors like task design, group composition, group norms, group cohesiveness and peer-group relationship affect leadership effectiveness and performance. If these factors are favorable, the leader will be effective.
4. *Organisational factors*—Organisational factors like organisational climate and organisational culture affect leadership effectiveness. If these are conducive, the leader will be effective.

Implications of the Theory

Situational theory has wide implications for managers. It

offers clues to why a manager, who is successful in one situation, fails when there is change in the situation. Therefore, the managers may do better by adopting management practices including leadership which match with the situational variables. In fact, the systems and contingency approach has become the way of thinking in management and leadership is no exception.

This theory, however, should not be taken as the final word in leadership. The theory appears to be good on the surface but becomes quite complex in practice because of the presence of numerous contingent factors. However, managers can overcome this problem by diagnosing these factors suitably. This is not necessarily provided by the theory but experience has a major role to play in this case.

There appears to be one more important lacuna in this theory. The theory loses the insight of leadership and the leader is overwhelmed by the contingent factors. In the following section we will discuss various leadership styles:

Leadership styles are the patterns of behaviour which a leader adopts for influencing the behaviour of followers or subordinates in any organisational setting. These patterns emerge in a leader's management style as one begins to respond in the same fashion under similar conditions. The leader develops habits of actions that become somewhat predictable to those who work with the person. Various researchers have proposed different leadership styles. These styles are either based on behavioural approach or situational approach of leadership. Some of the important theories or models which prescribe leadership styles are given below.

Leadership style based on behavioural approach:

- Power orientation.
- Leadership as a continuum.

— Employee-production orientation.

— Likert's management system.

— Managerial grid.

— Path-goal model.

Such a classification does not necessarily mean that a particular theory or model, grouped under one particular approach of leadership, does not consider the tenets of the other approach. Tenets of other approaches are also considered. However, such a consideration is secondary and the theory has not been built on such a consideration.

Power Orientation

Power orientation approach of leadership styles is based on the degree of authority which a leader uses in influencing the behaviour of his/her subordinates. Based on the degree of use of power, there are three leadership styles:

1. Autocratic leadership.
2. Participative leadership.
3. Free-rein leadership.

Autocratic Leadership

Autocratic leadership is also known as authoritarian or directive style. In autocratic leadership style, a manager centralises decision-making power in oneself. The person structures the complete situation for the employees and they do what they are told. Here, the leadership may be negative because followers are uninformed, insecure and afraid of the leader's authority. There are three categories of autocratic leaders:

1. *Strict autocrat*—A strict autocrat follows autocratic styles in a very strict sense. The method of

influencing subordinates' behaviour is through negative motivation, that is, by criticising subordinates, imposing penalty etc.

2. *Benevolent autocrat*—A benevolent autocrat also centralises decision-making power with oneself, but his/her motivation style is positive. The person can be effective in getting efficiency in many situations. Some people like to work under strong authority structure and they derive satisfaction through such a leadership style.
3. *Incompetent autocrat*—Sometimes superiors adopt autocratic leadership style just to hide their incompetence. This is because in other styles they may be exposed before their subordinates. Such a technique cannot be used for a long time.

The main advantages of autocratic technique are as follows:

1. There are many subordinates in the organisation who prefer to work under centralised authority structure and strict discipline. They get satisfaction from this style.
2. It provides strong motivation and reward to a manager exercising this style.
3. It permits very quick decisions as a single person takes most of the decisions.
4. Less competent subordinates also have scope to work in the organisation under this leadership style as they do negligible planning, organising and decision-making.

There are many disadvantages of autocratic leadership. They are as follows:

1. People in the organisation dislike it specially when it is strict and the motivational style is negative.

2. Employees lack motivation. Frustration, low morale and conflict develop in the organisation jeopardising the organisational efficiency.
3. There is more dependence and less individuality in the organisation. As such, future leaders in the organisation do not develop.

Considering the organisational efficiency and employee's satisfaction, autocratic style generally is not suitable.

Participative Leadership

This style is also called democratic, consultative or ideographic style. Participation is defined as mental and emotional involvement of a person in a group situation. This involvement encourages the person to contribute to group goals and share responsibility in them. A participative manager decentralises the decision-making process. Instead of taking unilateral decision, the person emphasizes on consultation and participation of the subordinates. Subordinates are broadly informed about the conditions affecting them and their jobs. This process emerges from the suggestions and ideas on which decisions are based. The participation may be either real or pseudo in nature. In case it is real, a superior gives credit to subordinate's suggestions and ideas in taking the decisions. In case it is pseudo, the superior preaches participation in theory, but the person will not prefer it in practice. There are various benefits of real participative management. These are as follows:

1. It is a highly motivating technique for employees. They feel elevated when their ideas and suggestions are given weight in decision-making.
2. The employees' productivity is high because they are party to the decision. Thus, they implement the decisions whole-heartedly.

3. They share the responsibility with the superior and try to safeguard the combined decisions. As the saying goes, a person who is sitting in a boat will never make a hole in it. The saying is applicable in this case.
4. It provides organisational stability by raising morale and attitudes of employees high and making them favourable. Further, leaders are also prepared to take organisational positions.

Keeping in view these advantages, management makes attempts to achieve effective participation. The common methods adopted are democratic supervision, committees, suggestion programmes and multiple-management. However, this style is not free from certain limitations. The limitations are as follows:

1. The complex nature of organisation requires a thorough understanding of its problems which lower level employees may not be able to do. In this case, participation does not remain meaningful.
2. Some people in the organisation want minimum interaction with their superiors or associates. For them, participation technique is discouraging instead of encouraging.
3. Participation can be used covertly to manipulate employees. Thus, some employees may prefer the open tyranny of an autocrat as compared to covert tyranny of a group.

Free Rein

Free rein or laisses-faire technique means giving complete freedom to subordinates. In this style, a manager determines the policy, programs and limitations for action. The entire process is left to the subordinates. Group members perform everything and the manager usually maintains contacts with outside persons to bring the information and materials which the group needs.

This type of style is suitable to certain situations where the manager can leave a choice to his/her group. This helps subordinates to develop independent personality. However, the contribution of manager is almost nothing. It tends to permit different units of an organisation to proceed at cross-purposes and can degenerate into chaos. Hence, this style is used very rarely in business organisations.

There are, in fact, a variety of styles of leadership behaviour between two extremes of autocratic and free rein. A broad range of styles on a continuum moving from authoritarian leadership behaviour at one end to free-rein behaviour at the other end. In latter years, a new pattern was developed for choosing the leadership behaviour. Because of changes in social system and organisational environment, the old continuum pattern is no longer valid. Organisations do not exist in vacuum, but are affected by changes that occur in the society. Thus, there would be more factors in situational variables affecting the leadership pattern. These forces lie outside the organisation interacting continuously with the organisational environment. Thus, new continuum of leadership pattern is more complex as compared to the previous one. In this pattern, the total area of freedom shared by manager and non-manager is constantly redefined by interaction between them and the forces in the environment. There is continual flow of interdependent influence among systems and people. The points on the continuum designate the types of manager and manager's behaviour that become possible with any given amount of freedom available to each. This continuum is more complex and dynamic reflecting the organisational and social realities.

A successful leader is one who is keenly aware of the forces that are more relevant to his/her behaviour at any given time. Such a leader accurately understands oneself, the individuals and the group one is dealing with. There is also an understanding of the organisation and the broader social environment in which the leader is operating.

However, merely understanding these factors correctly is not enough. A leader can be successful only when one is able to behave appropriately in the light of these perceptions and understanding. It is believed that a successful manager can be primarily characterised neither as a strong leader nor as a permissive one. The manager maintains a high batting average and accurately assesses the forces that determine the appropriate behaviour. This helps them to determine the behaviour pattern accordingly. Being both insightful and flexible; the manager is less likely to see the problem of leadership as a dilemma.

Employee-Production Orientation

The employee-orientation stresses the relationship aspects of employee's jobs. It emphasizes that every individual is important and takes interest in everyone. It accepts their individuality and personal needs. This is parallel to the democratic concept of leadership behaviour. Production-orientation emphasizes production and technical aspects of jobs. Employees are taken as tools for accomplishing the jobs. This is parallel to the authoritarian concept of leadership behaviour.

Almost at the same time, the leadership studies initiated by some university research scholars. They attempted to identify various dimensions of leader behaviour. Such studies identified two dimensions. These are as follows:

— Initiating structure

— Consideration

Initiating structure refers to the leader's behaviour in delineating the relationship between oneself and members of the work group. It endeavors to establish well-defined patterns of organisation, channels of communications, methods and procedures. Consideration refers to behaviour indicative of friendship, mutual trust, respect and warmth in the relationship between the leader and the members of the staff. The research studies also show that initiating structure and consideration are two distinct dimensions and not mutually exclusive. A low score on one does not necessitate high score on the other. Thus, leadership behaviour can be plotted on two separate axes rather than on a single continuum.

MANAGERIAL GRID

One of the most widely known approaches of leadership styles is the managerial grid. It emphasize that leadership style consists of factors of both task-oriented and relation-oriented behaviour in varying degrees. Their "concern for" phrase has been used to convey how managers are concerned about people or production, rather than "how much" production that goes out of the group. Thus, it does not represent real production or the extent to which human relationship needs are being satisfied. Concern for production means the attitudes of superiors towards a variety of things, such as, quality of decisions, procedures and processes, creativeness of research, quality of staff services, work efficiency and volume of output. Concern for people includes degree of personal commitment toward goal achievement, maintaining the selfesteem of workers, responsibility based on trust and satisfying inter-personal relations. The managerial grid identifies five leadership styles based upon these two factors found in organisations.

The five styles of managerial grid are as follows:

— Exertion of minimum effort is required to get work done and sustain organisational morale.

— Thoughtful attention to needs of people leads to a friendly and comfortable organisational atmosphere and work tempo.

— Efficiency results from arranging work in such a way that human elements have little effect.

— Adequate performance through balance of work requirements and maintaining satisfactory morale.

— Work accomplished is from committed people with interdependence through a common stake in organisational purpose and with trust and respect.

Each style points out the relative contents of concern for production or people. It implies that the most desirable leader's behaviour is 9,9. It represents maximum concern for production and people. Managerial grid is much similar to production-people orientation style as given by Ohio State University. However, there is one basic difference between the two. In managerial grid "concern for" is a predisposition about something or an attitudinal model that measures the predisposition of a manager. The Ohio State framework tends to be a behavioural model that examines how others perceive leader's actions.

Managerial grid is a useful device for a manager. It helps in identifying and classifying managerial styles. It helps a manager in understanding why he/she gets the reaction that one does from the subordinates. It can also suggest some alternative styles that may be available to the manager. However, it does not tell why a manager falls in one part or the other of the grid. A manager's style is influenced by many factors. This includes the kind of superiors, the subordinates and the business situation one is in. In managerial grid, the four comers and the midpoint of the grid are emphasized. These extreme positions are rarely found in their pure form in working conditions. In other words, a manager would more likely have a style of 8, 2 or 4, 6 or something similar. Nevertheless, managerial grid is widely used throughout the world as a means of managerial training and for identifying various combinations of leadership styles.

LEADERSHIP DEVELOPMENT

In management practices, an emphasis has been put on leadership development through training and development and by providing conducive work environment. The emphasis is on developing transformational leaders who can take care of changes which are occurring at much faster pace than before. Leadership development involves developing those qualities and attitudes in managers which help them to look into the future and to bring necessary change on proactive basis rather than on reactive basis. Leadership development is a means to an end; the end being successful change and competitive advantage. It has to have a context of pay-off. Alastair Robertson, a consulting partner on global leadership development practice with Anderson Consulting, suggest that leadership development should be considered on three levels. These are as follows:

1. The leadership of the business by the top team. It includes the explicit operation of the processes of leadership by this group.
2. The leadership of the top team by the CEO. It fully includes the dynamics of the top team effectiveness.
3. The personal development of individual executives as leaders.

Ingredients of Leadership Development

The ingredients of leadership depend on the characteristics that are critical for success in today's managerial context. According to Robertson, such characteristics are self-awareness, knowledge of one's own motivation, understanding and deploying one's own core capabilities and understanding how one affects others. All these characteristics help a person in the following ways:

1. A clear sense of capacity for and comfort with risk and change leads to an understanding of the role he/she should play in successful creation of experimental or developmental business elements.
2. A collaborative style, as opposed to one of control or of passive cooperation, leads to understanding of what is needed to create alliances that work
3. An understanding of multiple cultures and how to relate to diverse groups of partners, employees and customers leads to the ability to connect and work with a spectrum of styles. This includes those who find the task challenging.
4. A knowledge of strengths and weaknesses and the areas where the complementary skills and strengths of others can be brought to bear leads to the ability to let go. This is in the knowledge that the greater personal strengths of another will yield a better result.
5. Greater balance and reflection in life leads to energised workforces, retention of the best and brightest and reduced burnout.
6. Hardiness and resilience leads to an environment of learning quick recovery from errors and a workforce which can vigorously embrace the risks necessary to create the future.

7. Emotional competence generates and sustains trust, empathy, compassion and moral discernment.

Leadership Development Process

For inculcating the above characteristics, different routes may be adopted. In each route, various steps involved may be different. The following is the leadership development process adopted by Anderson Consulting:

1. Assess organisation's direction and current state. It also involves assessing the speed at which business results should be achieved and its implications for leadership.
2. Assess organisation's culture, define required shifts and create action plans for leaders to change the culture. This enables new business goals to be met.
3. Coach individual executives on personal behaviour, actions and communication. In this case, there is a direct contrast between what they do today and what is needed tomorrow.
4. Coach executive teams on individual leadership and effective teamwork.
5. Create executive communication strategies for key constituencies – board of directors, shareholders, employees, union officials, customers and suppliers.

LEADERSHIP AND MOTIVATION

Motivation is one of the most important factors affecting human behaviour and performance. Managers attach great importance to motivation in organisational setting. It is the core of management. Effective directing leads to effectiveness, both at organisational and individual levels. This requires the understanding of what individuals want from the organisation. It is important to mention here that the individual's wants are not fully identified in this case.

Today, virtually all people lay people and scholars. They have their own concept of motivation and they include various terms such as motives, needs, wants, drives, desires, wishes, incentives, etc. in defining motivation. Technically, the term motivation can be traced to the Latin word *movere,* which means "to move." In order to understand the concept of motivation, we have to examine three terms. These are as follows:

— Motive

— Motivating

— Motivation and their relationship

Motive—Based on the Latin word *movere,* motive or need has been defined as follows:

— "A motive is an inner state that energises, activates, or moves and that directs behaviour toward organisational goals."

Motive has also been described as follows:

— "A motive is restlessness, a lack, a yen and a force. Once in the grip of a motive, the organism does something to reduce the restlessness, to remedy the lack, to alleviate the yen, to mitigate the force."

Here, we can differentiate between needs and wants. Needs are more comprehensive and include both physiological and psychological desires. Wants are expressed in narrow sense and include only those desires for which a person has money and also the desire to spend the money to satisfy the wants. As we shall see later in this discussion, there are many psychological needs such as social needs, recognition needs, etc. These do not fall under the category of wants.

Based on the definition of motivation, we can derive its nature relevant for human behaviour in an organisation. Following characteristics of motivation clarify its nature:

1. *Based on motives*—Motivation is based on individual's motives which are internal to an individual. These motives are in the form of feelings that the individual lacks something. In order to overcome this feeling of something lacking, he/she tries to behave in a manner which helps in overcoming the feeling.
2. *Affected by motivating*—Motivation is affected in the manner in which the individual is motivated. The act of motivating channelises need satisfaction. Besides, it can also activate the latent needs in the individual, that is, the needs that are less strong and somewhat dormant and harness them in a manner that would be functional for the organisation.
3. *Goal-directed behaviour*—Motivation leads to goal-directed behaviour. A goal directed behaviour is one which satisfies the causes for which behaviour takes place. Motivation has profound influence on human behaviour. In the organisational context, it harnesses human energy to organisational requirements.
4. *Related to satisfaction*—Motivation is related to satisfaction. Satisfaction refers to the contentment experiences of an individual which he/she derives out of need fulfillment. Thus, satisfaction is a consequence of rewards and punishments associated with past experiences. It provides means to analyse outcomes already experienced by the individual.
5. *Person motivated in totality*—A person is motivated in totality and not in part. Each individual in the organisation is a self-contained unit and his/her needs are interrelated. These affect their behaviour in different ways. Moreover, feeling of needs and

their satisfaction is a continuous process. As such, these create continuity in behaviour.

6. *Complex process*—Motivation is a complex process. Complexity emerges because of the nature of needs and the type of behaviour that is attempted to satisfy these needs. These generate complexity in motivation process in the following ways:
   - *(i)* Needs are internal feelings of individuals and sometimes, even they, themselves, may not be quite aware about their needs and the priority of these. Thus, understanding of human needs and providing means for their satisfaction becomes difficult.
   - *(ii)* Even if needs are identified, the problem is not over. A particular need may result into different behaviours from different individuals because of their differences. For example, the need for promotion may be uniform for different individuals but all individuals may not engage in similar type of behaviour. They may adopt different routes to satisfy their promotion needs.
   - *(iii)* A particular behaviour may emerge not only because of the specific need but it may be because of a variety of needs. For example, hard work in the organisation may be due to the need for earning more money to satisfy physiological needs or may be to enjoy the performance of work itself. In this case, money becomes secondary and the motivation becomes to get recognition as a hard-working person.
   - *(iv)* Goal-directed behaviour may not lead to goal attainment. There may be many constraints in the situation which may restrain the attainment of goal directed behaviour. This may lead to

frustration in an individual creating many problems.

Types of Needs

There are many needs which an individual may have and there are various ways in which these may be classified. The basic objective behind classification of needs into different categories is to find out similarity and dissimilarity in various needs so that incentives are grouped to satisfy the needs falling under one category or the other. From this point of view, a meaningful classification of needs is based on the sources through which needs emerge. Needs may be a natural or biological phenomenon in an individual. These may also develop over a period of time through learning. Since these two types of needs emerge from two different sources, different types of incentives may satisfy these. Besides, there are certain needs which are neither purely biological nor these are completely learned. They fall in between the two. Therefore, a separate category has to be provided for these. Thus, needs may be grouped into the following three categories:

1. Primary needs
2. Secondary needs
3. General needs

Primary needs—Primary needs are also known as physiological, biological, basic or unlearned needs. The term primary is more comprehensive as compared to other terms. Primary needs are animal drives which are essential for survival. These needs are common to all human beings, though their intensity may differ. Some of the needs are food, sleep, air to breathe, satisfactory temperature, etc. These needs arise out of the basic physiology of life and are important to survival and preservation of species. These needs are also conditioned by social practices. According to the concept of economic man, these are the only wants of a human being. But researches in human behaviour show that psychological needs are equally important if not more important for human beings.

Secondary needs—In contrast to the primary needs, secondary needs are not natural but are learned by the individuals through experience and interaction. Therefore, these are also called learned or derived needs. Emergence of these needs depends on learning. This is the reason why we find differences among need pattern of a child and a matured individual. There may be different types of secondary needs like need for power, achievement, status, affiliation etc.

General needs—Though a separate classification for general needs is not always given, such a category seems necessary because there are a number of needs which lie in the grey area between primary and secondary classifications. In order to be included in this category, a need should not be learned. At the same time, it is not completely physiological either. This includes certain needs like need for competence, curiosity, manipulation, affection etc.

This classification of needs into different categories helps in providing an understanding of the way needs emerge. Their detailed description is provided in various theories of motivation, particularly based on contents. These theories try to explain the different needs which people seek to satisfy.

Motivation and Behaviour

Motivation causes goal-directed behaviour as indicated in its nature. Feeling of a need by an individual generates a feeling that he/she lacks something. This lack of something creates tension in the mind of an individual.

Since the tension is not an ideal state of mind, the individual tries to overcome this by engaging himself in a behaviour through which he/she can satisfy the needs.

Goal-directed behaviour leads to goal-fulfilment and the individual succeeds in fulfilling his/her needs and thereby overcomes tension in a favorable environment. Behaviour ends the moment tension is released. However, satisfaction of one-need leads to feeling of another need. This can include either the same need lapsing after certain time or different need emerging. This way the goal-directed behaviour goes on. Thus, goal-directed behaviour is a continuous process.

6

HOW TO CONTROL YOUR ORGANISATION

Planning and controlling are closely related to each other. If you do not decide on the targets and goals there is nothing for you to control i.e. if you do not know the direction in which to go where is the question of controlling. And remember, controlling is the basic function of every manager.

BASIC CONTROL PROCESS

The basic control process is fundamentally same for different things such as say office, sales, production, accounts etc. The basic control process consists of the following:

(a) Fixing a goal or a standard.

(b) Comparing the results with the goal or standard fixed.

(c) Taking corrective action for variations from the plan.

Fixing the Goals

As stated, controls are comparing the results with the plans. The first step in the controlling process is establishing the goals or targets or standards. There are many types of goal settings. Among the best are the verifiable goals or targets.

Comparing the Results

Comparing the results with the goals is as important as setting the goals itself. Comparison should be done with constructive intent and should be forward looking rather than finding fault. It is quite true that measuring the results is not always an easy task and appraisal of performance in such a situation is a huge task. The more difficult and complex it becomes to control, the more important it becomes to control.

Taking Corrective Actions

Corrective actions can be many. The managers should know exactly where to take corrective action. A manager can take corrective action as follows:

— Better leading.

— Reassignment.

— Redefining the duties.

— Adding staffs or better selection and training or even removing from the job.

— By re-planning the resetting the goals and targets.

As we have learnt that comparing the results is not easy, yet in order to have effective control, a manager should select the important points that are critical to performance and achieving the objectives and watching them closely. One of the more important control principles states that effective control requires attention to those factors critical to evaluation performance against plans. The ability to select critical points of control is an art in management science. Generally, the following are the critical points selected for close scrutiny:

(1) Capital standards.

(2) Cost standards.

(3) Revenue standards.

(4) Physical standards.

(5) Service standards.

(6) Targets itself as standards.

(7) Plans as standards.

(8) Break-even analysis.

1. *Capital standards*—There are different types of capital standards. The balance sheet will disclose the capital standards such as the ratios of current assets to current liabilities, debt to net worth, fixed investment to total investment, cash and receivables to payables and notes or bonds to stock, as well as the size and turnover of inventories.
2. *Cost standards*—These are financial values measurements such as direct costs, indirect costs, labour costs, material costs, selling costs etc.
3. *Revenue standards*—These are also financial values such as sales per capita or revenue per client etc.
4. *Physical standards*—These are non financial measurements such as the size, hardness, amount of fuel consumed per unit of time, production per unit time, sales unit per man per month etc.
5. *Services standards*—These are neither physical nor financial standards such as the quality of after sales service, installation service, breakdown service etc.
6. *Targets as standards*—As the name implies the targets itself can be set as standards.
7. *Plans as standards*—Plans also require control. Much importance is attached to strategic planning and therefore for success of the plan there should be

proper control. The advantage of strategic control is that one gets the real picture of the enterprise's performance.

8. *Break-even analysis*—It is the relation between the cost and profit. It is that point at which the cost and revenue of the enterprise are exactly equal. In other words, it is that point where the enterprise neither earns a profit nor incurs a loss.

CHARACTERISTICS OF CONTROL

A good effective control has some characteristics. They can be listed as follows:

1. *Forward looking*—The control should be forward looking with a view to guard the business against future dangers. It helps in taking corrective actions well in advance rather than wait for the situation to develop to the danger level before tackling them.
2. *Continuous process*—Controlling should be a continuous process.
3. *Flexible*—Controlling should be flexible and should match with the requirements of the organisation and the changing environment.
4. *Controlling at all levels*—Managers, at all levels, exercise control with varying degrees.
5. *Tailor made to suit individual plans and managers*—Controls should be designed to suit individual plans and manager and their personalities. For example, the budgets and various financial ratios have broad applications. One should be aware of the critical factors and they should be able to use techniques and information suited to them.

TYPES OF CONTROL

Organisations often use different standardised documents

to ensure that complete and consistent information is gathered. Documents include titles and dates to detect different versions of the document. Computers have revolutionised administrative controls through use of integrated management information systems, project management software, human resource information systems, office automation software, etc. Organisations typically require a wide range of reports. For example, financial reports, status reports, project reports, etc. These are used to monitor who is doing what, by when and how. This involves the use of different types of controlling techniques.

CONTROLLING TECHNIQUES

The control system will only be as effective as the techniques employed. Different techniques are used to control the activities of the enterprises. We shall now look at them. Broadly they can be classified as old and new techniques.

Old Techniques

In spite of emergence of newer techniques of control the traditional methods are still found to be very useful. They have been in use for a long time and so are still popular. The important techniques are budgeting, cost accounting or standard costing, financial statements, ratio analysis, break-even analysis, auditing, reports, rules and personal observation.

Budgeting

A budget is a statement of expected results during a given time period expressed in numerical terms either in financial or in non-financial terms. Revenue and expense and capital budgets are budgets in financial terms and materials, sales and production budgets are non-financial budgets. Budgets are also some times referred to as "Profit Plans."

Types of budgets

Depending on the need and purpose for which it is intended budgets can be classified as follows:

Revenue and expense budgets—These budgets consist of sales budgets, sales and distribution cost budgets, production budgets and production cost budgets. Sales forecasting is the foundation for sales budget. The sales manager prepares it with the assistance of his/her sales team. Sales budget is the basis of budgetary control since the revenue from the sales of products or services furnishes the principal income to pay operating expenses and yield profits. The selling and distribution cost budget includes the advertising cost, research and development cost, transport cost etc. The production budget lays down the quantity of units to be produced during the period. The production cost budget is subdivided into raw materials budget, labour budget, production overhead budget etc.

Capital expenditure budgets—These budgets outline the capital expenditures on the plants, machineries, equipments etc.

Cash budgets—This is one of the most important controls in business. It gives the expected receipts and payments for the period. It indicates the requirement of cash at various points of time and helps in planning and arranging cash to meet the needs of the business.

Master budgets—The master budgets, also known as budget summaries, give the summary of all the budgets and shows how they affect business as a whole. It provides detailed particulars regarding production, sales, cash fixed assets etc.

Merits

1. The deviations from the budget standards are found out and suitable corrective action can be taken in time.
2. Budgets improve communication.
3. Budgets make it possible to coordinate the work of the entire organisation.
4. The budget helps to learn from the past experience.

Demerits

1. Budgets deprive managers of the much-needed freedom in managing their activities.
2. Budgets may sometime become very cumbersome and unduly expensive.
3. Budgets are mostly inflexible and rigid and do not respond to internal or external environmental changes.
4. Some times budgetary goals become more important than enterprise goals.

Variable budgets—In order to overcome the rigidity of the budgets and build in maximum flexibility, variable budgets are widely used. The variable budget is based upon an analysis of expense items to determine how individual costs should vary with volume of output. Costs that vary with volume of output range from those that are completely variable to those that are only slightly. The task of variable budgeting involves selecting some unit of measure that reflects volume. It also includes inspecting the various categories of costs through different statistical methods, engineering analyses and other means for determining how these costs should vary with volume of output.

Another method of obtaining variable budgeting is to establish alternative budgets. Sometimes a company establishes budgets for a high level of operation, sometimes a medium level and at times a low level. The three budgets are approved for the company as a whole and for each organisational segment for 6 or 12 months in advance.

Budget flexibility is also obtained with a plan referred to as the supplemental monthly budget. Under this plan, a 6-month or 1-year budget is prepared for the primary purpose of outlining the framework of the company's plans, coordinating them among departments and establishing department objectives.

Zero-base budgeting—This is another type of budgeting and its purpose is similar to the purpose of a well-operated system of variable budgeting. By starting the budget of each program from base zero, costs are calculated afresh for each budget period. Thus avoiding the common tendency in budgeting of looking only at changes from a pervious period.

This technique has generally been applied to so-called support areas, rather than to actual production areas, on the assumption that there is some room for discretion in expenditures for most programs in such areas as marketing, research and development, personnel, planning and finance. The principal advantage of this technique is of course the fact that it forces managers to plan each program package afresh.

Cost Accounting or Standard Costing

Profit earned by the business to large extent, depends on the production cost. Standard costing is one the techniques of cost control and is being increasingly used by modern business concern for the purpose of cost reduction and cost control. The various steps involved in standard costing are as follows:

— Setting of cost standards for various components of cost.
— Measurement of actual performance.
— Comparison of actual cost wit h the standard cost laid down.
— Finding the variance of actual cost from the standard cost.
— Finding the causes of variance.
— Taking necessary action to prevent the occurrence of variance in future.

Financial Statements and Ratio Analysis

The trading profit and loss account and the balance sheet of a company are the usual financial statements that are prepared to indicate what financial events occurred during a specified period. Managers use these statements to compare their organisations with other organisations and can thus evaluate their own performance. In addition, people outside the organisation evaluate the organisation's strengths, weaknesses and also use the information.

Ratio analysis seeks to extract information from a financial statement in a way that allows an organisation's financial performance or condition to be evaluated. Some of the commonly used ratios are as follows:

(i) *Liquidity ratios:* They measure the company's ability to pay back short-term debts by converting assets quickly into cash.

(ii) *Debt ratios:* They measure the company's ability to pay back the long-term commitments.

(iii) *Profitability ratios:* These ratios express profits as percentage of sales or of total assets to depict the company's efficiency of operation.

(iv) *Operating ratios:* These ratios measure how efficiently the manufacturing and sales are being carried out.

(v) *Inventory turnover ratios:* These ratios measure how efficiently the assets of a company are being used and it is the ratio of Sales/Inventory.

(vi) *Total assets turnover ratios:* These are the measures of the effective use of the company's assets. It is expressed as sales or total assets.

Break-even Analysis

Break-even analysis can be used both as an aid in decision-making and as a control device.

New Techniques

We have till now seen the control techniques that have in use for a long time. However, of late, some more techniques have been used to control the efficiency of the organisations. These newer techniques are used in addition to the older techniques. In United States, the two of the major new ones are Programme Evaluation and Review Technique (PERT) and Critical Path Method (CPM). PERT was developed by the Special Projects Office of the US Navy and was first formally applied to the planning and control of the Polaris Weapon System in 1958 and in the launch of Sputnik. CPM is also a similar control technique that was jointly developed independently, virtually at the same time, by the engineers at the DU Pont Company and Remington Rand of USA. Although it is different in some aspects, it utilises the same principles. PERT is a method used to size a software product and calculate the Standard Deviation (SD) for risk assessment. The PERT equation (beta distribution) estimates the Equivalent Delivered Source Instructions (EDSIs) and the SD based on the analyst's estimates of the lowest possible size, the most likely size, and the highest possible size of each computer program component (CPC).

In non-mathematical terms, PERT is a time-event network analysis system in which the various events in a program or project are identified with a planned time established for each. These events are placed in a network showing the relationships of each event to the other events. Under both the techniques, a project is decomposed into activities and then all activities are integrated in a highly logical sequence to find the shortest time require to complete the entire project. The main difference between PERT and CPM lies in the treatment of time estimates. PERT was created primarily to handle research and development projects in which time spans are hard to estimate with any degree of accuracy. Consequently, PERT time spans are based on probabilistic estimates. CPM, on the other hand, is usually concerned with projects that the organisation has had some previous experience with. Time estimates, therefore, can be made relatively accurately.

Strengths and Weaknesses

There are five important advantages of PERT. First, it forces managers to plan, because it is impossible to make a time-event analysis without panning and seeing how the pieces fit together. Second, it forces planning all the way down the line, because each subordinate manager must plan the event for which he or she is responsible. Third, it concentrates attention on critical elements that may need correction. Fourth, it makes possible a kind of forward looking control; a delay will affect succeeding events and possibly the whole project unless the manager can make up the time by shortening the allocated to some action in the future. Fifth, the network system with its subsystems enables managers to aim reports and pressure for action at the right spot and level in the organisation structure at the right time. PERT also has certain limitations. These are as follows:

1. The technique is not useful when a program is nebulous and no reasonable, "guesstimates" of schedule can be made.
2. It has emphasis on time only and not on costs.
3. PERT has a limited application to one-time non-repetitive projects. It does not help control in continuous processing and production.

CONTROL PROCESS

The steps in control process are fundamentally same for different things. The basic control process, consists of the following:

— Fixing a goal or a standard.

— Comparing the results with the goal or standard fixed.

— Taking corrective action for the variations from the plan.

Most controls are designed for specific things. This includes policies, wages and salaries, employee selection and training, research and development, product quality, costs, pricing, capital expenditures, cash and other areas where we wish performance to conform to plans. Such controls are partial in the sense that they apply to a part of an enterprise and do not measure total accomplishments against total goals.

Many of the controls are based on feedback by measuring deviations from plans. Also, the traditional approach is to find out who is responsible for the undesirable deviation and to get that person to correct it. This is direct control. But, would it not be better to prevent undesirable deviations from occurring in the first place? Most people would answer the question with a yes. It is therefore recommended that preventive control be applied. This approach helps a highly qualified manager to make fewer mistakes and thus reduces the need for direct control.

Levels of Control Process

Planning and control are increasingly being treated as an interrelated system. Along with techniques for partial control, control devices have been developed for measuring the overall performance of an enterprise, its integrated division or a project against overall goals. There are many reasons for control of overall performance. It is important that planning should apply to enterprise of major division goals just as overall controls are applied.

Decentralisation of authority, especially in product or territorial divisions, creates semi-independent units and these should be subjected to overall controls to avoid the chaos of complete independence. An overall control permits measuring an intergraded area manager's total effort rather than parts of it.

Many overall controls in business are, as one might expect, financial. Business owes its continued existence to profit making; its capital resources are as scarce and a life-giving element. Since finance is the binding force of business, financial controls are certainly an important objective gauge of the success of plans.

Financial measurements also summarise, as a common denominator, the operation of a number of plans. Further, they accurately indicate total expenditures of resources in reaching goals. This is true in all forms of enterprise. Although the purpose of an educational or government enterprise is not to make monetary profits, any responsible manager should have some way of knowing what goal achievement has cost in terms of resources. Proper accounting is important not only for business but for government as well.

Financial controls, like any other control, have to be tailored to the specific needs of the enterprise or the position. Doctors, lawyer and managers at different organisational levels do have different needs for controlling their area of operation. Financial analyses also furnish an excellent window through which accomplishment in non-financial areas can be seen. A deviation from panned costs, for example, may lead a manager to find the causes in poor planning inadequate training of employees or other non-financial factors.

A widely used control of overall performance takes the form of a summary of budgets. A budget summary, being a resume of all the individual budgets, reflects company plans so that sales volume, costs, profits, utilisation of capital and return on investment may be seen in their proper relationship. In these terms it shows top management how well the company as a whole is succeeding in meeting its objectives.

For the best control through a budget summary, a manager must first be satisfied that total budgets are an accurate and reasonably complete portrayal of the company's plans. The manager should study the budget reports and any material accompanying them to determine whether the comparison of budget and actual costs shows the real nature of any deviations. For example, a company head criticised his factory manager for being considerably over his labour budget in a month when the labour force had been materially reduced and the temporary increase in expenses was due to severance pay. Minor discrepancies should receive appropriately little attention. The purpose, of a control system is to draw attention to important variations, and both the budget reports and the attention paid to them should reflect this. Above all, a manager should never forget that a budget summary is no substitute for profitable operation. Budgeting is never more perfect than the planning behind it, and plans—especially long-range plans—are subject to the imperfections caused by change and uncertainty. There may even be times when a manager must forget the budget and take special action to meet unexpected events. Budgets are meant to be tools, and not masters, of managers.

On the other hand, managers should not underestimate the value of budget summaries in providing an effective means for overall control in situations of decentralised authority. Budget summaries furnish a means whereby enterprise objectives can be clearly and specifically defined and departmental plans can be made to contribute toward such objectives. Should the budget summary and the reports of actual events indicate that the enterprise as a whole is not tending toward its objectives, top managers have a convenient and positive means of finding out where the deviations are occurring. The summaries, thus, furnish a useful guide for corrective action.

Profit and Loss Controls

The income statement for an enterprise as a whole serves important control purposes, mainly because it is useful for determining the immediate revenue *or* cost factors that have accounted for success or failure. Obviously, if it is first put in the form of a forecast, the income statement is an even better control device in that it gives managers a chance, before things happen, to influence revenues, expenses, and consequently profits.

Since the survival of a business usually depends on profits and since profits are a definite standard against which to measure success, many companies use the income statement for divisional or departmental control. Because it is a statement of all revenues and expenses for a given time, it is a true summary of the results of business operations. Profit and loss control, when applied to divisions or departments, is based on the premise that if it is the purpose of the entire business to make a profit, each part of the enterprise should contribute to this purpose. Thus, the ability of a part to make an expected profit becomes a standard for measuring its performance.

Profit and loss control usually is practicable only for major segments of a company since the paperwork involved in building up profit and loss statements for smaller departments tends to be too heavy. Also, profit and loss control usually implies that managers of a division or department have fairly wide authority to run their part of the business as they see fit, with profit the primary standard of success. However, many companies that do not decentralise authority have nonetheless found profit and loss control valuable. The focus on profit and the sensitivity of the organisational unit to it are worthwhile even when managers have limited independence in seeking profit as they wish.

Profit and loss control suffers its greatest limitation from the cost of the accounting and paper transactions involving intra-company transfer of costs and revenues. Profit and loss control also may be inadequate for overall performance. Top managers may not wish to give their division managers too much authority, and they may desire the additional assurances of good budgetary control. In addition, profit and loss control in and of itself does not provide a standard of desirable profits or policy controls in the area of product-line development or in other matters of long-term overall company concern.

Another limitation of profit and loss control, especially if it is carried very far in the organisation, is that departments may come to compete with an aggressive detachment not helpful to enterprise coordination. On the other hand, in many companies there is not enough feeling of departmental responsibility for company profit, and departments may develop the smugness of a monopolist with an assured market. The assembly department, the manufacturing or the service department that can force its output on the sales department should buy the parts fabrication department that knows its products, and the engineering group that has a monopolistic hold on both production and sales are dangerous monopolists indeed. Profit and loss control can break down these islands of monopoly So, in spite of limitations—and especially if accompanied by an intra-company pricing policy which requires that departments meet competitive prices of suppliers outside the enterprise, rather than a policy which is based on cost—profit and loss control can give top managers an extraordinary measure of overall control.

Return on Investment Control

One of the most successfully used control techniques is that of measuring both the absolute and the relative success of a company or a company unit by the ratio of earnings to investment of capital. The return-an-investment approach, often referred to simply as ROI, has been the core of the control system. A large number of companies have adopted it as their key measure of overall performance. This yardstick is the rate of return that a company or a division can earn on the capital allocated to it. This tool, therefore, regards profit not as an absolute but as a return on capital employed in the business. The goal of a business is seen, accordingly, not necessarily as optimising profits but as optimising returns from capital devoted to business purposes. This standard recognises the fundamental fact that capital is a critical factor in almost any enterprise and, through its scarcity limits progress. It also emphasizes the fact that the job of managers is to make the best possible use of assets entrusted to them.

Advantages of ROI

One of the principal advantages of using return on investment to control overall performance is that it, like profit and loss control, focuses managerial attention on the central objective of the business. This helps in making the best profit possible on the capital available. It measures the efficiency of the company as a whole and of its major divisions or departments, its products and the planning. It takes attention away from mere increase in sales volume or asset size or even from the level of costs and it draws attention to the combination of factors that promotes successful operation.

Another advantage of control by return on investment is that it is effective where authority is decentralised. It not only is an absolute guide to capital efficiency but also offers the possibility of comparing efficiency in the use of capital within the company and with other enterprises. By holding departmental managers responsible for performance in terms of the rupees invested in their parts of the business, it forces them to look at their operations from the point of view of top management. Managers often insist on heavy capital investments for new equipment or drive for lower prices to increase sales without taking into account the possible effect of their requests on the company as a whole.

A further advantage of return-on-investment control, if it is complete and shows all the factors bearing upon the return, is that it enables managers to locate weaknesses. If inventories are rising, the rate of return will be affected or if other factors camouflage inventory variations and leave the rate looking good, tracing back influences will disclose any weakness of the inventory situation and open the way for consideration of a remedy.

Disadvantages of ROI

With all its advantages and its widespread use by well-managed and successful companies, this method of control is not foolproof. Difficulties involve availability of information on sales, costs, and assets and proper allocation of investment and return for commonly sold or produced items. Does the present accounting system give the needed information? If not, how much will it cost to get it through either change in the system or special analyses? If assets are jointly used or costs are common, what method of allocation between divisions or departments should be used? Should a manager be charged with assets at their original costs, their replacement costs or their depreciated values?

Setting up a return-on-investment control system is no simple task. Another question is, what constitutes a reasonable return? Comparisons of rates of return are hardly enough, because they do not tell the top manager what the rate of return should be. Perhaps as good a standard as any is one that meets or surpasses the level of competing firms, since, in a practical sense, the best tends to be measured not by an absolute level but by the level of the competition for capital.

One of the dangers of overemphasis on the rate of return is, that may lead to undesirable inflexibility in investing capital for new ventures. Many companies using this important measuring tool have set minimum rates which a division, new-product programme, or investment should meet before the allocation of additional capital would be approved.

Perhaps the greatest danger in return-on-investment control, as with any system of control based on financial data, is that it can lead to excessive preoccupation with financial factors within a firm or an industry. Undue attention to ratios and financial data can cause a firm to overlook environmental factors such as social and technical developments. It might also lead a company to overlook the fact that capital is not the only scarce resource with which a business can grow, prosper, and endure. Competent managers, good employee moral, good customer and public relations are scarce resources. A well-managed company would never regard any financially based control as the sole gauge of overall performance.

Various Approaches to Control

At the basis of control is the fact that the outcome of plans is dependent on the people who carry them out. For instance, a poor educational system cannot be controlled by criticising its product, the unfortunate graduate; a factory turning out inferior products cannot be controlled by consigning products to the scrap heap; and a firm plagued with customer complaints cannot be controlled by ignoring the complainers. Responsibility for controllable deviations lies with whoever has made unfortunate decisions. Any hope of abolishing unsatisfactory results lies in changing the future actions of the responsible person, through additional training, modification of procedures, or new policy. This is the crux of controlling the quality of management.

There are two ways in which responsible people modify future action. The normal procedure is to trace the cause of an unsatisfactory result back to the persons responsible for it and get then to correct their practices. This may be called direct control. The alternative in the area of management is to develop better managers who will skillfully apply concepts, techniques and principles and who will look at managing and managerial problems from a systems point of view, thus eliminating undesirable results caused by poor management. It is also known as preventive control.

Let us have a look at the direct control. Every enterprise has many standards to compare the actual output of goods or services in terms of quantity, quality, time and cost with plans. A negative deviation indicates in terms of goal achievement, cost, price, personnel, labour-hours or machine-hours. In this case, performance is less than good or normal or standard and results do not conform to the plans.

The causes of negative deviations will often determine whether control measures are possible. Although an incorrect standard may cause deviations, if the standard is correct, plans may fail because of the following reasons:

- Uncertainty
- Lack of knowledge
- Lack of experience
- Lack of judgment on the part of those who make the decisions or take actions.

Managerial errors caused by unforeseeable events cannot be avoided. The fixing of personal responsibility by direct control techniques is of little avail in such situations.

If the cause of error is poor judgment, whether due to inadequate training, to lack of experience, or to failure to use appropriate information in decision-making, corrections can be made. Managers can improve their education, be transferred to acquire broader experience, or be cautioned to take better stock of the situation before making decisions.

Preventive Control

The principle of preventive control embraces the idea that most of the responsibility for negative deviations from standards can be fixed by applying fundamentals of management. It draws a sharp distinction between analysing performance reports, essential in any case, and determining whether managers act in accordance with established principles in carrying out their functions. The principle of preventive control, then, can be stated as follows:

The higher the quality of managers and their subordinates, the less will be the need for direct controls.

The extensive adoption of preventive control should await a wider understanding of managerial principles, functions, and techniques as well as management philosophy.

While such an understanding is not achieved easily, it can be gained through university training, on-the-job experience, coaching by a knowledgeable superior, and constant self-education. Moreover, as progress is made in appraising managers as managers, preventive control can be expected to have more practical meaning and effectiveness.

7

COMMUNICATION SKILLS

Communication establishes relationships and makes organising possible. Every message has a purpose or objective. The sender intends—whether consciously or unconsciously—to accomplish something by communicating. In organisational contexts, messages typically have a definite objective i.e. to motivate, to inform, to teach, to persuade, to entertain, or to inspire. This definite purpose is, in fact, one of the principal differences between casual conversation and managerial communication. Effective communication in the organisation centers on well-defined objectives that support the organisation's goals and mission. Supervisors strive to achieve understanding among parties to their communications.

COMMUNICATION PROCESS

Communication is the process of passing information and understanding from one person to another. The communication process involves six basic elements. These are sender (encoder), message, channel, receiver (decoder), noise, and feedback. One can improve communication skills by becoming aware of these elements and how they contribute to successful communication. Communication can break down at any one of these elements.

Non-verbal Communication

Non-verbal messages include images, actions and behaviours used to communicate. Images include photographs, film, charts, tables, graphs, and video. Non-verbal behaviours include actions, body language, and active listening. Actions and body language include eye contact, gestures, facial expressions, posture, and appearance. The effective communicator maintains eye contact for four to five seconds before looking away. Gestures should be natural and well timed. Grooming and dress should be appropriate for the situation. Listening requires good eye contact, alert body posture, and the frequent use of verbal encouragement.

The grapevine consists of rumours and gossip. The supervisor should pay attention to the grapevine, but should not depend on it for accurate information.

Active Listening

Active listening is a way of listening and responding to another person that improves mutual understanding. Often when people talk to each other, they do not listen attentively. They are often distracted, half listening, half thinking about something else. When people are engaged in a conflict, they are often busy formulating a response to what is being said. They assume that they have heard what their opponent is saying many times before, so rather than paying attention; they focus on how they can respond to win the argument.

Active listening is a structured form of listening and responding that focuses the attention on the speaker. The listener should take care to attend to the speaker fully, and then repeats, in the listener's own words, what he or she thinks the speaker has said. The listener does not have to agree with the speaker. He or she should simply state what they think the speaker said. This enables the speaker to find out whether the listener really understood. If the listener did not, the speaker can explain some more.

Be other-directed; focus on the person communicating

Follow and understand the speaker as if you were walking in their shoes. Listen with your ears but also with your eyes and other senses.

Be aware of non-verbally acknowledge points in the speech

Let the argument or presentation run its course. Don't agree or disagree, but encourage the train of thought.

Be involved

Actively respond to questions and directions. Use your body position (e.g. lean forward) and attention to encourage the speaker and signal your interest.

Paraphrasing

It is restating a message, but usually with fewer words. Where possible try and get more to the point.

Purpose

- To test your understanding of what you heard.
- To communicate that you are trying to understand what is being said. If you're successful, paraphrasing indicates that you are following the speaker's verbal explorations and that you're beginning to understand the basic message.

When listening consider asking yourself:

- What is the speaker's basic thinking message
- What is the person's basic feeling message

Clarifying

It is a process of bringing vague material into sharper focus.

Purpose

- To untangle unclear or wrong listener interpretation.
- To get more information
- To help the speaker see other points of view
- To identify what was said

Perception Checking

It is the request for verification of your perceptions.

Purpose

- To give and receive feedback
- To check out your assumptions

Studies from over twenty-five years of experience with non-directive interviewing in industry have produced a series of guides for emphatic listening. For a manager the most useful of these guides are:

1. Listen patiently to what the other person has to say, even though you may believe it is wrong or irrelevant. Indicate simple acceptance, not necessarily agreement, by nodding or perhaps injecting an occasional "mm-hmm" or "I see."
2. Try to understand the feeling the person is expressing, as well as the intellectual content. Most of us have difficulty talking clearly about our feelings, so it is important to pay careful attention.
3. Restate the person's feeling briefly, but accurately. At this stage you simply serve as a mirror.

Encourage the other person to continue talking. Occasionally make summary responses such as, "You think you are in a dead-end job", or "You feel the manager is playing favourites." In doing so, keep your tone neutral and try not to lead the person to your pet conclusions.

4. Allow time for the discussion to continue without interruption and try to separate the conversation from more official communication of company plans. Do not make the conversation any more "authoritative" than it already is by virtue of your position in the organisation.
5. Avoid direct questions and arguments about facts; refrain from saying, "That is just not so", "Hold on a minute, let's look at the facts", or "Prove it." You may want to review evidence later, but a review is irrelevant to how a person feels now.
6. When the other person touches on a point you want to know more about, simply repeat his statement as a question. For instance, if he remarks, "Nobody can break even on his expense account", you can probe by replying, you say no one breaks even on expenses?" With this encouragement he will probably expand on his previous statement.
7. If the other person appears to genuinely want your viewpoint, be honest in your reply. In the listening stage, try to limit the expression of your views since these may influence or inhibit what the other person says.
8. Do not get emotionally involved yourself. Try simply to understand first and defer evaluation until later.
9. Be quiet. Let the other person talk. Actively listen to what they have to say.

The Voice

The voice is probably the most valuable tool of the presenter. It carries most of the content that the audience takes away. One of the oddities of speech is that we can easily tell others what is wrong with their voice, e.g. too fast, too high, too soft, etc., but we have trouble listening to and changing our own voices. There are four main terms used for defining vocal qualities:

Volume

Volume is how loud the sound is. The goal is to be heard without shouting. Good speakers lower their voice to draw the audience in, and raise it to make a point.

Tone

Tone is the characteristic of sound. An airplane has a different sound than leaves being rustled by the wind. A voice that carries fear can frighten the audience, while a voice that carries laughter can get the audience to smile.

Pitch

How high or low a note is?

Pace

This is how long a sound lasts. Talking too fast causes the words and syllables to be short, while talking slowly lengthens them. Varying the pace helps to maintain the audience's interest.

The Body

Your body communicates different impressions to the audience. People not only listen to you, they also watch you. Slouching tells them you are indifferent or you do not care...even though you might care a great deal! On the other hand, displaying good posture tells your audience that you know what you are doing and you care deeply about it. Also, a good posture helps you to speak more clearly and effective.

Throughout you presentation, display.

Eye contact

This helps to regulate the flow of communication. It signals interest in others and increases the speaker's credibility. Speakers who make eye contact open the flow of communication and convey interest, concern, warmth, and credibility.

Facial expressions

Smiling is a powerful cue that transmits happiness, friendliness, warmth, and liking. So, if you smile frequently you will be perceived as more likable, friendly, warm, and approachable. Smiling is often contagious and others will react favourably. They will be more comfortable around you and will want to listen to you more.

Gestures

If you fail to gesture while speaking, you may be perceived as boring and stiff. A lively speaking style captures attention, makes the material more interesting, and facilitates understanding.

Posture and body orientation

You communicate numerous messages by the way you talk and move. Standing erect and leaning forward communicates that you are approachable, receptive, and friendly. Interpersonal closeness results when you and your audience face each other. Speaking with your back turned or looking at the floor or ceiling should be avoided as it communicates disinterest.

Proximity

Cultural norms dictate a comfortable distance for interaction with others. You should look for signals of discomfort caused by invading other's space. Some of these are: rocking, leg swinging, tapping, and gaze aversion. Typically, in large rooms, space invasion is not a problem. In most instances there is too much distance. To counteract this, move around the room to increase interaction with your audience. Increasing the proximity enables you to make better eye contact and increases the opportunities for others to speak.

Vary your voice

One of the major criticisms of speakers is that they speak in a monotone voice. Listeners perceive this type of speaker as boring and dull. People report that they learn less and lose interest more quickly when listening to those who have not learned to modulate their voices.

8

NEGOTIATION SKILLS

Negotiation is usually considered as a compromise to settle an argument or issue to benefit ourselves as much as possible. Communication is always the link that will be used to negotiate the issue/argument whether it is face-to-face, on the telephone, or in writing. Remember, negotiation is not always between two people; it can involve several members from two parties.

There are many reasons why you may want to negotiate and there are several ways to approach it. We all have our own point of views. And these viewpoints form the basis of our goals and objectives. Each time you communicate with a potential client, vendor or employee, you exchange ideas and information. However, your goals are likely to differ. Negotiation, in essence, is the art of compromise. Negotiation skills are vital to the success or failure of your interactions, and ultimately, your goals. Negotiating is one of the key tools you can use to accomplish your goals.

PILLARS OF NEGOTIATION WISDOM

Relationship

What impact will this negotiation have on our personal relationship with other negotiators or our constituents, the parties who stand to gain or lose depending on the negotiation's outcome?

Interests

What are the reasons that drive our pursuit of particular objectives, and can another party's ideas or resources help serve our interests better than what we bring to the table?

BATNA

Our Best Alternative To a Negotiated Agreement (BATNA) may be derived from resources we control or influence. We may have choices of parties with whom to negotiate or may be better off relying on ourselves. BATNAs can change during negotiation each time we learn a new piece of information.

Creativity

Are we to be governed by standard operating procedure, or can our interests be better served by thinking out of the box? If our ideas are the only ones worth taking seriously, it is hard to justify bringing additional parties into a negotiation—the decision-making process.

Fairness

Do we feel as if we are being treated fairly? How do other parties feel? If a negotiator feels he or she is not being dealt with in a fair manner, he or she may agree for purposes of bringing the bargaining to a close, but may walk away without having bought into the agreement.

Commitment

Negotiations can only be called successful if they lead to agreements the parties are committed to fulfil. Learn whether the people at the bargaining table have the capacity to keep the promises they make.

Communication

Information is the fundamental asset in negotiation. We communicate best by listening. We should keep asking ourselves whether the negotiation process is being used as a successful way of communicating information.

By considering which of these deserves more attention in a given negotiation before the negotiation process begins, we are likely to do a better job. The recent past may have presented some shocks, but to be a good negotiator, you have to accept that things may not always go the way you expect. Keep the "seven pillars" in mind, and you should be able to respond wisely to the circumstances you face.

ESSENTIALS OF A SUCCESSFUL NEGOTIATION

Know what "you" want

Think through exactly what you want. Be specific and have valid reasons for why you need it. Knowing what you want, and why, will help you to be clearer and more confident.

Know what "they" want

Before you start negotiating, it is important to have an idea of what the other party would like the outcome to be, too. So think it through why do they need what you are offering/asking for? And do your research on how can you make them feel like they have got a good deal?

Be Fair

If what you are asking for is fair and justifiable, e.g., you would like to earn as much as someone you work equally as hard as, then you are much more likely to get what you want.

Believe you are worth it

You have to believe that you deserve your desired outcome. If you do not, the moment your client or boss questions you, your argument will fall apart because you do not have enough confidence in it. Believe it, trust yourself, and rehearse it.

Listen Carefully

When your boss/client is talking to you during negotiations, do not use that time to plan your next line of attack. It is more important that you listen to them and see their point of view. They will take you more seriously if you do, even if you disagree with them.

Keep it Friendly

Negotiating is not about confrontation. It is about two parties reaching an amicable, mutually beneficial agreement. Keep that in mind when you are talking and, even if you do not get what you want this time, view it as good practice for the future.

Have an Alternative

When you are discussing specifically what you want, as well as what they want, work out what you would be prepared to walk away with if you are not successful.

9

STAFFING AND RECRUITING

The managerial function of staffing is defined as filling, and keeping filled, positions in the organisation structure. This includes identifying work-force requirements, inventorying the people available and recruiting, selecting, placing, promoting, appraising, planning the careers of, compensating and training or otherwise developing both candidates and current jobholders to accomplish their tasks effectively and efficiently. In other words, human resource management encompasses those activities designed to provide, motivate and coordinate the human resources of an organisation.

There is a saying that the company he keeps knows a man and similarly the people it is comprised of know an organisation. Without competent people, organisations will either pursue inappropriate goals or find it difficult to achieve the desired goals.

Human dynamics play an important role in surmounting obstacles, defusing complex situations and achieving organisational goals. It is because of this reason that some organisations succeed in spite of major obstacles, environmental changes and challenges, while others crumble rather quickly under external pressures.

STAFFING

In the fast changing environment, globalisation, competition, increased opportunities and career orientation and many other factors have made the traditional approach to personnel management obsolete. The present situation demands a complete and strategic approach to HRM. HRM strategy must fit in the overall strategy of the organisation because it involves long-term implications. The modern approach to the management acknowledges the interest of the employees – the major stakeholders of the organisation. Every step in HRM is of great importance and of them selection decisions stands out to be the most important. Selection decision can be sub divided into the following functions:

— Determining the nature of the job to be filled

— Determining the type of personnel required

— Determining the sources of recruitment

— Determining the selection process

The first step in 'placing the right man in the right job at the right time' is determining the nature of the job to be performed. In order to do the HR manager must consult the concerned line manager and find out the specific nature of the job. Once the job profile has been made, the characteristics of the candidate to fill in the job should be determined. The next step is to decide the source from which we can procure the right people. This could be either be from within the organisation or from outside.

RECRUITMENT

A good recruitment plan has the following basic elements:

— Job profile

— Job specification

— Recruitment source

Recruitment can be defined as the process of locating, identifying and attracting prospective and capable employees to the organisation.

Job Description

Before the employees can be recruited, the manager must have a clear idea about the activities and responsibilities required in the job being filled. Therefore job analysis is an early step in the recruitment process. The accuracy of the individual specification and of all the subsequent stages in selection will depend on the quality of the job analysis. Therefore it is important to have it right.

A meeting between the person responsible for selection and the head of the relevant department is necessary to decide the following:

1. The key characteristics of the job and the people who will fill it.
2. A time schedule for selection, based on the urgency with which the vacancy has to be filled up.
3. How the exercise has to be handled–internal/ external.
4. The terms and conditions on which the job will be filled.

Once the job description has been determined and accompanying hiring or person specification is developed. Hiring or person specification defines the education, experience, skills that an individual should have in order to perform effectively in the position. The characteristics specified should be relevant. Only those, which are demonstrably connected with success or failure in the job, should be specified and independent. Any over lapping elements should be avoided and assessable. The attributes that can be assessed with the selection tools available should be included.

In the recruitment process, the HR department normally has primary responsibility for ensuring compliance with the mass of legislation and subsequent legal decisions concerning discrimination. Access discrimination refers to hiring considerations and practices that are based on the candidate's membership in a particular population subgroup and not related in any way to present or future job performance. Treatment discrimination involves practices unrelated to job performance that treat subgroup members differently from others once they are in the work force. Ultimately, however, the human resources department must instruct and educate managers in the implications of compliance for their respective departments. Even job titles can be sexist and reflect de facto discrimination. For example, the job titles foreman and salesman are now outmoded. Many companies have replaced them with supervisor and salesperson, respectively.

In recent years, a host of social issues are affecting both recruitment and management more and more. The use of drug testing, AIDS testing, computer surveillance and even genetic screening by many companies has stirred fears among workers and other that employers are delving too far into worker's personal lives.

Sources of Recruitment

Recruitment takes place within a labour market. This includes a mass of available people who have the skills to fill open positions. Sources for recruitment depend on the availability of the right kinds of people in the local labour market as well as on the nature of the positions to be filled. An organisation's ability to recruit employees often hinges as much on the organisation's reputation and the attractiveness of its location as on the attractiveness of the specific job offer. In general, the sources of employment can be classified into the following two types:

— Internal

— External

Many organisations have a policy of recruiting or promoting from within except in very exceptional circumstances. Filling a job opening from within the organisation has the following advantages:

— Individuals recruited from within are already familiar with the organisation and its members and this knowledge increases the likelihood they will success.

— A promotion from within fosters loyalty and inspires greater effort among organisation members.

— It is usually less expensive to recruit or promote from within than to hire from outside the organisation.

The disadvantages of the internal recruitment are as follows:

— The obvious limitations of available talents.

— It may encourage complacency among the employees who assume promotions.

— It reduces the chances of fresh viewpoints entering the organisation.

Selection

Once the recruiting effort has developed a pool of candidates, the next step in the HRM process is to determine who is best qualified for the job. This step is called the selection process. Selection involves mutual decision and prediction. The enterprise decides whether to make a job offer and how attractive the offer should be. The job candidate decides whether the enterprise and the job offer fit his or her needs and personal goals. The process also seeks to predict which applicants will be successful if hired. Success, in this case, means performing well on the criteria the enterprise uses to evaluate employees.

Correct selection decisions are those where the candidate was predicted to be successful in advance and prove to be successful on the job. At times the applicant is predicted to be unsuccessful and, as expected, performs unsatisfactorily after getting selected. While in the first case, we the worker is successfully accepted, in the later the worker is successfully rejected.

Errors arise when we reject a candidate who would have performed successfully on the job. This is termed as reject error. In certain situations a worker is accepted ultimately and performs unsatisfactorily. This is called accept errors. Both the above errors can be minimised if the system is impartial, has a degree of objectivity and follows a fairly uniform standard of assessment. A skilled manager should understand the benefits of good selection and also should be aware of the cost of poor selection decision.

Steps in the Selection Process

There are broadly four steps in the selection process and each step can further be subdivided depending on the need. These are as follows:

1. *Screening of application forms:* Application forms are wealth of information and should be used wisely. It should be interpreted correctly. The primary objective would be to eliminate applicants failing to meet minimum qualifying requirements.
2. *Tests:* These include tests of intelligence, aptitude, ability and interest. Tests in intellectual ability,

(iv) *Personality tests*—This test is of great importance and should be conducted for all posts. Individuals possessing intelligence, aptitude and experience for a certain job have often been found unsuccessful because of their inability to get along with others. Some of the personality tests are given below:

— *Thematic apperception test (TAT)*— This is one of the most popular projective tests in which the candidate is shown a series of pictures, one at a time and asked to write a story for each of the pictures. Examples of such scenes are, an old man knocked down by a car or a schoolboy sleeping under a tree with his school bag and knife lying beside him. The psychologist analyses the story in terms of such factors as length, vocabulary, bizarre ideas, plot, mood, etc.

— *Rorschach inkblot test*—In this test the candidate is asked to organise unstructured ink blots into meaningful concepts. An integrated picture of the candidate's personality is then formulated.

3. *Interview:* Interviews are designed to probe into areas that cannot be addressed by the application form or tests. These areas usually consist of assessing candidates' motivation, ability to work under stress, inter-personal skills and ability to fit-in the organisation. The use of the interview in selecting executives makes sense whereas for most lower level jobs appears questionable.

4. *Selection decision:* In practice, the final decision will probably be between three or four candidates. It is unlikely that any of the three or four remaining applicants meet the person specification in every way. The personnel specialist together with line management will now have to weigh up the

strengths and weaknesses of each candidate. The right decision depends on management judgement.

Recruitment and selection is vital function of HR in the organisation. Slightest mistake will lead to a square peg in round hole. Instead of following a blind elimination process, focus should be on selecting people based on the skills and competencies required for the job.

SOCIALISING, TRAINING AND DEVELOPMENT

Like every individual, every organisation too has a unique personality. Every new employee needs to know the organisation and its culture well to become effective at work. The culture is the system of shared values and beliefs within an organisation and guides the behaviour of its members.

Strong work culture helps the organisation to realise its business goal easily and effectively. Culture includes longstanding and often, unwritten rules and regulations. It has a special language that facilitates communication among members, shared standards of relevance regarding the critical aspects of the work that is to be done, matter-of-fact prejudices, standards for social etiquette and demeanour. It also includes established customs for how members should relate to peers, subordinates, superiors and outsiders and other traditions that clarify to members about the appropriate and smart behaviour within the organisation.

This calls for giving proper orientation to the new employees on socialising norms to shape their behaviour and actions in line with the philosophy and culture of the organisation. This is basically molding people to internalise the systems and practices of the organisation to feel comfortable with. A new employee irrespective of his knowledge and competencies needs to understand, appreciate and acclimatise himself with the culture of the organisation.

Upon entry into a new job or a new organisation, all employees initially need to learn how things are done in the new environment. This includes things they cannot find in any policy and procedure manual. Moreover, new hires may have insufficient skills and technological changes may require new job skills. Job redesign sometimes also requires the employees to learn more skills. The employees who are transferred or promoted may need to acquire new skills and knowledge. A new product could also require technologies not used earlier by employees or changes in company strategy may mean that senior management needs to adopt new leadership behaviour and acquire new business knowledge. In some cases, the need for socialisation, training and development can be immediate. While in other cases, the future needs can be anticipated and planned. When done well, socialisation creates intensely loyal employees. Companies that have perfected the socialisation process include IBM, Wal-Mart, Procter and Gamble and Nestle.

Socialisation may occur at different phases. The new employees may have to learn company values and organisational folklore, including the importance of product quality and the dedication and commitment of the retired employees. This intense socialisation results in increased commitment to the success of the company, willingness to work for long hours and decreased absenteeism and employee turnover. Moreover, an employee takes pride in identifying himself with the organisation which has its past glory to share.

Socialisation, in an organisational context, is basically a process of adaptation to a new culture of the organisation. The term refers to all the processes undergone by employees. For instance, when one begins a new job or accepts a lateral transfer or get a promotion, one is required to understand the new dynamics and unwritten practices that exist which helps in making adjustments. One should adapt to a new environment, different work activities, a new boss, a different group of co-workers and probably a different set of standards for what constitutes a good performance. Employee socialisation, training and development are an organisation's intentional efforts to improve current and future performance by increasing capabilities.

It is not unusual to confuse a new employee's initial orientation on the job with the socialisation process. In reality, orientation is only a small part of the overall socialisation of a new organisation member.

Orientation involves in introducing a new employee to the activities of the organisation and to his (or her) work unit to make him more comfortable and effective in the new environment. It helps the new entrants to get rid of their apprehensions, anxiety and unknown feeling in a new organisation. A good orientation program familiarises the new member with the organisation's objectives, history, philosophy, procedures and rules. It communicates relevant human resource policies such as hours of work, pay procedures, overtime requirements, fringe benefits, review the specific duties and responsibilities of the new member's job, provide information on the organisation's physical facilities and introduce the employee to his or her superior and co-worker. Orientation program may or may not be a formal exercise with a systematic schedule of activities to be undertaken.

Normally, large organisations have a very systematic program drawn for the new entrants which they follow religiously as they give maximum importance to this activity. However, in many small organisations this is done more informally. Socialisation can be conceptualised as a process made up of the following three stages:

— Pre-arrival
— Encounter
— Metamorphosis

The process impacts on the new member's work productivity, commitment to the organisation's objectives and his or her decision to stay with the organisation. The pre-arrival stage explicitly recognises that each individual enters with a set of values, attitudes, and expectations of their own. In case of experienced people, they come with the cultural mindset of their previous organisation. In both the cases, it is essential to acclimatise them with the culture, values and functioning of the new organisation. A fresher, who comes directly from the campus, only has conceptual knowledge and some of the information regarding the functioning of the organisation during the classroom teaching. In practice, most of the things are completely different which may not match with the expectation of these fresher. In the selection process, organisations try to look for candidates who could adapt to the culture and requirements of the organisation. Hence, the candidates who correctly anticipate the expectations of the employer are likely to be picked up by the organisation. In this process, the candidate tries to understand and learn about the organisation from different sources to make himself/herself suitable for the job.

Upon joining the organisation, the new employees enter the encounter stage. At this stage, the individuals confront with the reality which may be just the reverse to their expectations about their job, their co-workers, their boss and the organisation in general. If expectations prove to be more or less accurate, the encounter stage merely provides a confirmation of the perception gained earlier. In reverse situation, there is a culture shock that needs to be managed. In this case, the experienced people need to unlearn before they learn new values, philosophies and culture. If this is not done properly, then the individual may feel suffocated and incline to quit the job.

The new members should work out any problems discovered during the encounter stage. This may mean going through changes. Hence, we call this the metamorphosis stage. We can say that the metamorphosis is complete when the new members have become comfortable with the organisation and their job. They have internalised the norms and practices of the new organisation and their work groups. The new members feel accepted by their peers as trusted and valued individuals. They are self-confident that they have the competence to complete their job successfully. They understand the system and especially their own tasks. They also understand the rules, procedures and informally accepted practices.

Orientation

Orientation is a process, as mentioned earlier, of acquainting the new employees with the existing culture and practices of the new organisation. It includes the activities of introducing a new employee to the organisation and the work unit. The focus of orientation is to make the induction process smooth in breaking initial anxieties of the new recruits. This involves a gamut of activities like familiarising the new members with the organisation's objectives, history, philosophy, procedures and rules. This also includes communicating to them relevant HRM policies such as work hours, pay procedures, overtime requirements, company benefits and at the same time reviewing the specific duties and responsibilities for the job as well as organisation's physical facilities offered to the employees. Introducing the employee to his or her manager and co-workers is also an important part of orientation.

During any orientation, it is important to convey that organisation believes in continuous learning and improvement. A well-planned programme, though requires sincere effort, expenditure and more time, it always pays substantially to the individual employee and the organisation in terms of performance. The first encounter in job is essentially crucial in developing a good or bad experience. Hence, they should get all the support while passing through this transition phase. The way they are treated can help them in making a smooth transition to their new organisation, or can cause them unnecessary anxiety. Many employees report feeling confused and lost during their first weeks at work, not knowing where to go for information or help. Superiors and colleagues can influence the new employee's learning, motivation, productivity, satisfaction and retention with a good orientation program. Designing and developing a program needs to focus on the content, approach and people to be involved in delivering the content. A sequential, layered program with various staff members sharing responsibility for orientation seems to work the best.

The presence and the interaction of the CEO in the orientation program is a very important activity. This boosts the morale of the new employees that they are important in the organisation. Moreover, the experience shared by the CEO helps the participant to understand the mission-vision strategy of the organisation and also the leadership style prevailing in the organisation. The address of the CEO, being the top executive of the organisations, normally impacts the new entrants which helps in molding them to the new culture.

Orientation Process

It is essential to orient a person with the system, practices and culture of the organisation. It is the most difficult proposition because one needs to unlearn many past experience and mindset of the participants to prepare them to learn the new things. Orientation as a process has the following three stages:

1. A general orientation.
2. A departmental orientation.
3. A specific job orientation.

General orientation—In this phase, the basic objective is to make the employee feel at ease and comfortable and to motivate him/her to go through the orientation process seriously to adapt properly to the organisation. This part should include exposing them to the history of the organisation, business goals and processes of the organisation. They should be taken for a visit to the whole organisation to understand the business processes. The classroom input should be given and after that they should be placed in each department as a trainee to understand the processes and also to appreciate that each activity is important in the organisation for the final outcome.

It is essential to create team spirit among the newcomers by assigning different team based assignments. The new work force, during the orientation, should be treated with dignity and respect. They should not be treated as strangers to the organisations. Senior executives should be invited to address the newcomers to share their experiences and also to interact with them in formal as well as informal ways. This helps the newcomers to gain confidence and feel motivated. It is essential to draw an alignment between the organisational goal and the individual goal. The organisation's goal should be dearly explained to the newcomers so that they can draw the relevance out of it for them. These initiatives ensure an effective orientation program for the new incumbents and also reduce the initial apprehensions which in turn helps in developing trust, cooperation and motivation.

Orientation to a department—The individuals are oriented to their department where they are going to work. The role, responsibility of the individual in the department and the departmental operating practices need to be told to the new incumbent. Initially the employees should be exposed to each and every activity of the department for a couple of months to understand the activities involved and to develop an acquaintance with the superiors, peers and subordinates. It is only later that they should be assigned any specific job.

Orientation to a specific job—A specific assignment, with a job description, may be given to the individual. The person needs to be oriented with the methodology to be adopted for a particular job. This means that the role involved in that particular job has to be clearly stated and also the role expectation of the significant others has to be communicated to the incumbent. The superior if required should adapt a hand holding approach to guide the person in the role.

Training and Development

Training may be defined as a planned program designed to improve performance and to bring about measurable changes in knowledge, skills, attitude and social behaviour of employees for doing a particular job. Nowadays, training has an additional purpose of facilitating change. And management training is basically equipping managers with such knowledge, skills and techniques as are relevant to managerial tasks and functions.

Today and tomorrow's training programmes should focus on soft-skills such as interpersonal communication, teamwork, innovation and leadership. Most importantly, the training has to be comprehensive, systematic and continuous. It should be closely linked to the strategy with which the company is planning to fight the competition. In the future, it is training that acts as catalyst between people, between strategy and systems, between customers and the organisation.

Irrespective of whether we are involved in employee training or employee development, the same result is required. Training for employee development is different in terms of approach and the teaching required. Training is basically the learning experience that brings a permanent change in an individual, thereby improving his/her ability to perform on the job. Learning is mostly the modification of behaviour in the light of past experience which is a continuous process to keep the employees competent and good performer. The principles of learning are as follows:

1. *Initial motivation or readiness*—The initial urge drives the individual to learn. Hence, a need, a wish or an ambition is required to motivate the individual to learn. Though learning is a learner's responsibility, the initial motivation needs to be created by the organisation.
2. *Multiple response or response by trial and error*—Learning may take place either in a single trial or through multiple trials. The length of the provisional trial and error period depends on the content of the task, the maturity of the learner and the skill, understanding and experience which the person brings to the task. The basic objective of the training is to reduce the trial and error period and to help the learner to master the skills quickly and effectively.

3. *Selection of responses through reinforcement or the law of effect*—The provisional trial period ends when the correct activity occurs. The right response is reinforced and thereby increases the chances of their subsequent selection and repetition. On the other hand, the response that is not reinforced drops out. This is the law of effect.
4. *Principle of extinction*—It is important to drop out the responses that are not reinforced. This reduction of occurrence is called extinction. Extinction bears somewhat the same relationship to reinforcement that forgetting does to frequent recall. Hence, reinforced learned skills, though temporarily forgotten, may reappear suddenly.
5. *Law of exercise in habit formation*—Once the correct sequence of acts has been established as a result of reinforcement, the skills can be learnt through repetition or exercise.

The quality of employees and their development through training and education, are major factors in determining long-term profitability of a small business. If you hire and keep good employees, it is wise to invest in developing their skills so they can increase their productivity. Training is often considered only for new employees. This is many times a mistake because ongoing training for senior employees helps them to update themselves of the rapidly changing job requirements.

Purpose of Training and Development

The people development in the organisation has been emphasized because of the following advantages:

- Creating a pool of readily available and adequate replacements for personnel who may leave or move up in the organisation.

— Enhancing the company's ability to adopt and use advances in technology because of a highly knowledgeable staff.

— Building a more efficient, effective and highly motivated team which enhances the company's competitive position and improves employee morale.

— Ensuring adequate human resources for expansion into new programmes.

Employees frequently develop a greater sense of self-worth, dignity and well being as they become more valuable to the firm and to the society as a whole. Generally, they will receive a greater share of the material gains that result from their increased productivity. These factors give them a sense of satisfaction through the achievement of personal and company goals.

Training Methods

There are two main types of training. These are as follows:

— On the job techniques

— Off the job techniques

Individual circumstances together with questions such as what and why of the training program determine the type of method that is used.

On the job training is basically learning by doing while one is already working. Training is imparted to employees while they perform their regular jobs. In this method, they do not lose time while they are learning. After a plan is developed for training, employees should be informed of the details. A timetable should also be prepared with periodic evaluations to inform employees about their progress. On-the-job training includes coaching, orientations, job instruction training, apprenticeships, internships and assistantships, job rotation and coaching.

Off-the-job is imparted outside the work premises. This includes classroom activities such as lectures, special study, films, television conferences or discussions, case studies, roleplaying, simulation, programmed instruction and laboratory training. The four most popular off-the-job development techniques are as follows:

- Sensitivity training
- Transactional analysis
- Lecture courses
- Simulation exercises

Techniques of Training

The process of sensitivity training became quite popular during the 1950's. It is a method of changing behaviour through group processes. It is often referred to as laboratory training. It influences the participants through unstructured group interaction. Members are brought together in a free and open environment in which participants discuss themselves and their interaction process is loosely facilitated by a professional behavioural scientist. This scientist creates opportunity for the participants to express their ideas, beliefs and attitudes. He or she does not accept or overtly reject any leadership role. The objectives of sensitivity training are as follows:

- To provide managers with increased awareness of their own behaviour and how others perceive them.
- Greater sensitivity to the behaviours of others.
- Increased understanding of group processes.

Certain specific results that are expected out of the training are increased ability to empathise with others, improved listening skills, greater openness, increased tolerance for individual differences and improved conflict resolution skills.

Transactional analysis (TA)—When people interact with others, there is a transaction for which a person responses to another. The study of these social transactions between people is called transactional analysis (TA). The analysis was popularised by Berne's book *Games People Play* and Harris's book *I am ok, you are ok.* According to Berne, two people interact with each other from one of the three psychological positions known as ego states. These three states are called parent, adult and child. People, whose parent ego state is in control, may be protective, controlling, nurturing, critical and instructive. They may dogmatically refer to the policies and standards. The adult ego state will appear as rational, calculative, factual and unemotional behaviour. It tries to upgrade decisions by seeking facts, processing data, estimating probabilities and holding factual discussions. The child ego state reflects the emotions developed in response to childhood experiences. It may be spontaneous, dependent, creative or rebellious. Like a child, this ego state desires approval from others and prefers immediate rewards. The objective of TA is to provide better understanding of how people relate to one another so that they may develop improved communication and human relations.

Lecture courses—Formal lecture courses offer an opportunity for managers or potential managers to acquire knowledge and develop their conceptual and analytical abilities.

Simulation exercises—The widely used simulation exercises include decision games and role-playing. Role-playing and simulation are training techniques that attempt to bring realistic decision-making situations to the trainee. The problems generally encountered and alternative solutions are presented for discussion. Experienced employees can describe real world experiences and can help in developing the solutions to these simulations. This method is cost effective and is used in marketing and management training.

Simulated decision games and role-playing exercises puts individuals in the role of a decision-maker for sorting out managerial problems. Games provide opportunities for individuals to make decisions and to consider the implications of a decision on other segments of the organisation.

The advantages of simulation include the opportunities to create an environment similar to real situations that the managers face. It helps in avoiding the high costs involved that incurs in case the actions prove undesirable. The main disadvantage is the difficulty in duplicating the pressures and realities of actual decision-making on the job. It is believed that individuals often act differently in real-life situations than they do in acting out a simulating exercise.

Case study—Case analysis approach to management development was very popularised in some Business Schools. Taken from the actual experiences of organisations, these cases describe as accurately as possible, real problems that managers have faced. Trainees study these cases to determine problems, analyse causes, develop alternative solutions, select what they believe to be the best solution and implement it. Case study can provide stimulating discussions among participants, as well as excellent opportunities for individuals to defend their analytical and judgmental abilities. It appears to be a rather effective method for improving decision-making abilities within the constraints of limited information.

Coaching—When a manager takes an active role in guiding another manager, this activity is referred to as coaching. The effective coach, whether in any sports or in the corporate hierarchy, gives guidance through direction, advice, criticism and suggestions in an attempt to aid the growth of the employee. The technique of engaging managers for coaching other managers has certain advantages attached with it. It ensures learning by doing and creates opportunities for high interaction and rapid feedback on performance. The method has two specific disadvantages. These are as follows:

— Its tendencies to perpetuate the current managerial styles and practices in the organisation.

— Its heavy reliance on the instructor to become a good teacher.

Just as we recognise that all excellent sprinters do not make outstanding coaches, for the same reason we cannot expect that all excellent managers will be effective coaches. An individual can become a good manager without necessarily possessing the knack of creating a proper learning environment for others to do the same. Thus, the effectiveness of this technique relies on the ability of the coach.

Understudy assignments—The term understudy assignment includes potential managers who are given the opportunity to relieve an experienced manager of his or her job. They are allowed to act as a substitute during the leave period the manager. This term also describes providing assistance to positions as well as temporary opportunities to assist managers in completing their jobs.

This method works best in those organisations where managers recognise that their own promotion and advancement depend on preparing underlining to satisfactorily move into their jobs. The understudy, who is given the job for a short period of time, is given the opportunity to see the job in totality. While there are opportunities for sizeable errors, the technique is used predominantly in situations where major or critical decisions can be delayed until the manager returns or can be made in close consultation with the manager next up in line.

Job rotation—Job rotation involves moving an employee through a series of jobs, so that he can get a good feel for the tasks that are associated with different jobs. It is usually used in training supervisors. It represents an excellent method for broadening the manager or potential manager and of turning specialists into generalists. This can either be horizontal or vertical. Vertical rotation is nothing more than promoting a worker into a new position. Horizontal rotation is better understood as lateral transfer.

In addition to increasing the manager's experience and allowing the manager to absorb new information, it can reduce boredom and stimulate the development of new ideas. It can also provide opportunities for a more comprehensive and reliable evaluation of the manager by his or her supervisors. Additionally, since job rotation permits a greater understanding of other activities within the organisation, people are prepared more rapidly to assume greater responsibility, especially at the upper strata. As one moves up the organisation, it becomes increasingly necessary to understand the intricacies and interrelationships of activities. These abilities can be more quickly acquired by moving about within the organisation. Moreover, it helps in developing multi-skill approach in the organisation. The drawbacks of this method are as follows:

— Increased development costs
— Reduced productivity by moving a worker into a new position just when his or her efficiency at the

previous position has started creating organisational economies.

— Job rotation can also demodulate intelligent and aggressive trainees who seek specific responsibility in their chosen field.

Apprenticeship—This method helps develop employees who can do many different tasks involving several related groups of skills that allow the apprentice to practice a particular trade. The training takes place over a long period of time when the apprentice works for, and with, the senior skilled worker. Apprenticeships are especially suitable for jobs requiring production skills.

Internships and assistantships—These are usually a combination of classroom and on the job training. They are often used to train prospective managers or marketing personnel. Programmed learning, computer-aided instruction and interactive video have common features. They allow the trainee to learn at his or her own pace. Also, they allow material already learned to be bypassed in favour of material which is posing difficulty for the trainee. After the introductory period, the instructor need not be present and the trainee can learn at a self-controlled pace. These methods surely have a lot of advantages. However, smaller companies may not be able to afford the resources needed for them.

Training Needs in a Changed Marketplace

In a changed economic set-up with fierce competition companies rely on their strategy of beating rivals with new products, new designs and new methods of selling. These companies have to teach teamwork and streamlined production techniques to their employees. On the quality platform, companies have to train their workers in developing the mindset and culture for quality without which the whole effort can fail. Those companies, which choose to compete on the strength of their innovation, have to train their employees on creativity and lateral thinking. Companies trying to cut costs are compelled to train their employees in problem solving techniques. In the case of companies that globalise in order to expand their markets, find cross-cultural training for their managers a vital imperative.

PERFORMANCE APPRAISAL

Organisations are run and steered by people. It is through people that goals are set and objectives realised. The performance of an organisation is, thus, dependent upon the sum total of the performance of its members. An organisation is like a tune. It is not constituted by individual sounds but by their synthesis. The success of an organisation, therefore, depends on its ability to accurately measure the performance of its members and use it objectively to optimise them as vital resources.

The performance of an employee is his resultant behaviour on task which can be observed and evaluated. It refers to the contribution made by an individual in the accomplishment of organisational objectives. Performance can be measured by combining quantity, quality, time and cost. People do not learn unless they are given feedback on the results of their actions. For learning to take place, feedback should be provided regularly and it should register both successes and failures. It should also follow soon after the relevant action or actions. Performance appraisal system provides management an opportunity to recall as well as give feedback to people. This feedback is pertaining the performance of the worker. This helps them to correct their mistakes and acquire new skills.

Performance appraisal (PA) refers to all those

procedures that are used to evaluate the personality, the performance and the potential of its group members. Evaluation is different from judgment. The former is concerned with performance and the latter is concerned with the individual. While evaluation deals with achievement of goals, a judgement has an undercurrent of personal attack and is likely to evoke resistance.

Performance appraisal could be informal or formal. Informal performance appraisal is a continuous process of feeding back information to the subordinates about how well they are doing their work in the organisation. The informal appraisal is conducted on a day-to-day basis. For example, the manager spontaneously mentions that a particular piece of work was well performed or poorly performed. It is due to the close connection between the behaviour and the feedback on it, the informal appraisal quickly encourages desirable performance and discourages undesirable performance before it becomes permanently ingrained. Therefore, informal appraisal should not be perceived merely as a casual occurrence but as an important activity and an integral part of the organisation's culture. The formal performance appraisal occurs usually annually on formal basis and involves appraise and appraiser in finding answers to the following questions:

1. What performance level has to be achieved during the period?
2. Has it been achieved?
3. What has been the shortfall and constraints?
4. What are we going to do now?
5. How will we know that we have done it?
6. What kind of feedback can be expected?
7. What assistance can be expected to improve

performance?

8. What rewards and opportunities are likely to follow from the performance appraisal?

When the employees have this type of information, they are aware of the following specifications:

1. What the organisation expects from them?
2. What assistance is available?
3. What can they expect when the required level of performance is achieved?

This increases employee acceptance of the appraisal process and results in the trust that the employee has in the organisation. An environment that affords an opportunity for further growth while minimising stressful situations certainly enhances appraisal acceptance. Establishing this type of environment goes far beyond the performance appraisal process. Every aspect of managing people and their work relates to the improvement of their quality of work life. Performance appraisal is an integral part of a trusting, healthy and happy work environment that goes a long way in promoting the same.

Performance appraisal has been used for the following three purposes:

— Remedial
— Maintenance
— Development

A performance appraisal needs to cover all these three purposes with the same focus. If any purpose predominates, the system becomes out of balance. For instance, if remedial purpose is foremost, then the performance appraisal may become a disciplinary tool, a form of a charge sheet and a tool of power instead of instrument of evaluation. Sometimes maintenance becomes the main objective for an organisation. In this case, the process may become short, skimped and per functionary ritual. If there is too much emphasis on development, then the focus falls on the future assignment rather than on the current job.

Objectives of Performance Appraisal

Performance appraisal serves the following management objectives:

1. *Providing basis for promotion/transfer/termination*—Identifying those subordinates who deserve promotion or require lateral shift (transfer) or termination and can be used for career planning.
2. *Enhancing employees' effectiveness*—Helping employees in identifying their strengths and weaknesses. Also, informing them about the performance expected from them. This helps them to understand their role well and increases their efficiency at work. The feedback reinforces good performance and discourages poor performance. This also involves identifying employee's training and development needs. Identifying training and development needs of employees is necessary to prepare them for meeting challenges in their current and future employment.
3. *Aiding in designing training and development programs*—Identifying skills that need to be developed. This helps in tailor-making training and development programmes.
4. *Removing work alienation*—Counseling employees corrects misconceptions which might result in work alienation. Performance appraisal also helps employees in internalising the norms and values of the organisation.

5. *Removing discontent*—Identifying and removing factors responsible for worker's discontent motivates them for performing better at work. Performance appraisal helps in creating a positive and healthy work environment in the organisation.
6. *Developing interpersonal relationship*—Relations between the superiors and subordinates can be improved through realisation that there exists a mutual dependence. This mutual dependence leads to better performance and success. By facilitating employees to do introspection, self-evaluation and goal setting, their behaviour can be modified. Better interpersonal relationships lead to team building.
7. *Aiding wage administration*—Performance appraisal can help in development of scientific basis for reward allocation, wage fixation, raises, incentives etc.
8. *Exercising control*—Performance appraisal also provides a means for exercising control.
9. *Improving communication*—Performance appraisal serves as a mechanism for communication between superiors and subordinates.

Operation Performance Appraisal System

The introduction of performance appraisal should be planned during the development stage. The main steps are to train everyone on performance appraisal, and once in operation, to monitor and evaluate how the system is performing in practice.

Training

The importance of thorough training for both appraisers and appraisee, in the skills required to carry out performance appraisal effectively, cannot be overemphasized. Both parties in the performance appraisal process need guidance and training in the preparation of the following:

- Performance agreements and plans
- Conducting performance reviews
- Completing review forms

There is also a need to develop skills required to conduct appraisal discussions, including interpersonal skills.

Training can be provided by formal courses or workshops. It is probably best to develop a series of training modules, as it might be difficult to get people to go through all the training required at one time. It is believed that people are unable to absorb information at one go. The modules could consist of the following:

- Introduction to performance appraisal system
- Defining key tasks and setting objectives
- Working with attributes and competence
- Preparing performance and development plans
- Conducting appraisal discussions
- Rating
- Providing feedback
- Coaching and counseling.

10

PERFORMANCE MANAGEMENT

The aim of performance management is to establish a culture in which individuals and groups take responsibility for the continuous improvement of business processes, and of their own skills and contributions. Performance management systems can also be used as an integrating process, which meshes various human resource management activities with the business objectives of the organisation. They identified two broad thrusts towards integration.

— Reward-driven integration, which emphasises the role of performance payment systems in changing organisational behaviour and tends to undervalue the part played by other human resource development (HRD) activities.

— Development-driven integration, which stresses the importance of ensuring that appropriate HRD activities are in place to meet the long-term objectives of the organisation and, furthermore, to ensure business needs and HRD are coordinated. Although performance pay may operate in these organisations, it is perceived to be complementary to HRD activities, rather than dominating or driving them.

The specific aims of performance management are to:

- Achieve sustainable improvements in the organisational performance;
- Enable individuals to develop their abilities, increase their job satisfaction and achieve their full potential to their own benefit and that of the organisation as a whole;
- Develop constructive and open relationships between individuals and their managers in a process of continuing dialogue, which is linked to the work actually being done throughout the year;
- Provide a framework for the agreement of objectives as expressed in targets and standards of performance, so that mutual understanding of these objectives and the role both managers and individuals have to play in achieving them, is increased;
- Provide for the accurate and objective measurement and assessment of performance in relation to agreed targets and standards, so that individuals receive feedback from managers on how well they are doing;
- On the basis of this assessment, to enable individuals with their managers to: agree improvement plans and methods of implementing them, and jointly review training and development needs and agree how they should be satisfied;
- Provide an opportunity for individuals to express their aspirations and concerns about their work;
- Provide a basis for rewarding people in relation to their contribution by financial and/or non-financial means—the former consisting of performance related pay, and the latter including recognition of

achievement and opportunities to take on more responsibility or enhance knowledge and skills.

EFFECTIVE PERFORMANCE MANAGEMENT PROCESS

There are some important issues for the success of the installed performance systems. They are as follows:

Achieving the Business Strategy

An effective performance management system should develop employees' understanding of what needs to be achieved, help them to improve corporate performance and reward them on the basis of their contribution. The objectives set for senior managers are directly related to what they and the division, function, unit or department they control need to achieve to contribute fully to the attainment of corporate strategies. Senior managers in turn agree objectives with the members of their management team, spelling out the contribution the latter are expected to make in enabling their division, function etc to meet its targets.

This process is repeated at each level of the organisation, so that the objectives agreed there are consistent with those agreed for the next higher layer. This provides for a link between the objectives set for office and shop floor workers, and other employees, who are responsible for basic organisational activities and those set at corporate level.

Fulfilling Organisational Responsibilities

Besides setting clear corporate objectives and individual or team targets, this requires the implementation of a policy of human resource development, which provides for coaching, counselling and training on a continuing basis.

Enabling Employees to Manage their own Performance and Development

Performance management is not just a system driven by management to manage the performance of their employees. Rather it is a process, which enables employees to manage their own performance and development within the framework of clear objectives, and standards, which have been agreed with their managers. This does not absolve management from their responsibility to 'empower' employees through counseling and training. But it does place people in a situation where they are more in control of the consequences of their actions. This can increase their sense of responsibility. It also helps them to achieve what Maslow refers to as 'self actualisation'.

Management by Agreement

The essence of the performance management process is that it is a partnership between managers and the individuals who are members of their teams. This means that at every stage the aim is to obtain agreement on objectives, on the means of measuring performance, on the assessment of results and the factors affecting them, and on development and performance improvement plans.

Role of the HR Function

The HR function can stimulate the introduction of a performance management system and facilitate its development. It provides the training required and monitors its implementation. Fundamentally, however, a performance management system should be owned and driven by line managers and their staff.

Importance of Objectives

It enables employees to know what is required of them and on what basis their performance and contribution will be assessed. Objectives should:

— be jointly agreed in advance between the manager and the individual as both realistic and challenging and, as such, they are 'owned';

— measure the actual level of achievement so that the basis on which performance is assessed can be understood in advance and is as clear as possible;

— support the overall business strategies of the company so that the objectives, taken together, are mutually supportive and consistent throughout the organisation.

Input, Process, Output, Outcome Model

Performance management is concerned with:

— Inputs - The skills, knowledge and personal characteristics the individual applies to the job;

— Process - How the individual behaves in carrying out the task;

— Outputs - What is produced by the individual when the task has been completed;

— Outcomes - The impact of what has been achieved by the individual's performance on the results of the team, unit, function and, ultimately, the organisation. Outcomes are therefore defined by the effect an individual's contribution has beyond his or her particular job.

The distinction between inputs, process, outputs and outcomes can be illustrated by reference to the job of a training manager, one of whose objectives is to plan and deliver a new training programme. Performance on this task would be measured by reviewing:

- Inputs - The knowledge and skill deployed by the training manager in planning the course;
- Process - The effectiveness with which training skills were used in conducting and evaluating the course;
- Outputs - The quality of the courses themselves, in terms of their content, presentation and administration;
- Outcomes - The impact made by the training on the performance of participants.

Performance appraisal systems traditionally concentrated on inputs and, to a certain degree, process. They asked managers to assess personality traits and behaviour under such headings as initiative; willingness and relationships with people. The problem was that the ratings were highly subjective—there were no standards for exercising judgments on these characteristics. Managers were asked to 'play at being God' and they were not good at it.

Performance management systems emphasise the importance of outcomes, which the individual influences, as well as immediate outputs. They analyse inputs and processes to determine development and training needs, and provide the basis for performance improvement plans. They will be concerned with diagnosing correctly whether differential performance is a function of the individual's motivation or is a result of his or her ability. The way, in which people are managed, the resources they are given and the external factors beyond their control are also taken into account.

PROCESS OF PERFORMANCE MANAGEMENT

Performance management implies a marked shift in the relationship between managers and their staff. The manager is faced with a new and more challenging situation: counselling skills; effective listening; good communication; and the ability to handle and encourage upward appraisal all come to the fore. In essence, the development of a performance management system leads directly on to the need for a more systematic approach to skills-based management development.

The Process of Performance Management

Step 1. From the business plan, identify the requirements and competences required to carry it out.

Step 2. Draw up a performance agreement, defining the expectations of the individual or team, covering standards of performance, performance indicators and the skills and competences people need.

Step 3. Draw up a performance and development plan with the individual. These record the actions needed to improve performance, normally covering development in the current job.

They are discussed with job holders and will cover, typically:

— The areas of performance the individual feels in need of development.

— What the individual and manager agree is needed to enhance performance.

— Development and training initiatives.

Step 4. Manage performance continually throughout the year, not just at appraisal interviews done to satisfy the personnel department. Managers can review actual performance, with more informal interim reviews at various times of the year.

(*a*) High performance is reinforced by praise, recognition, increasing responsibility. Low performance results in coaching or counselling (*b*) Work plans are updated as necessary.

(*c*) Deal with performance problems, by identifying what they are, establish the reasons for the shortfall, take control action (with adequate resources) and provide feedback.

Step 5. Performance review. At a defined period each year, success against the plan is reviewed, but the whole point is to assess what is going to happen in future.

Organisations are introducing such systems for much the same reason as they pursued management by objectives. In other words, they are aiming to:

— Tie in individual performance with the performance of the organisation.
— Indicate where training and development may be necessary.

This plan + do – review cycle is the basic process of people management. It operates at two levels:

— *The macro level*—The management of the year's activity.
— *The micro level* – The development of performance through involvement at the doing stage.

PLANNING PERFORMANCE MANAGEMENT

Performance management systems can promise more than they achieve. They can fail for four main reasons:

1. Top management is not fully behind the scheme;
2. Line management feels it is a waste of time and/or mishandle the objective-setting and review processes;
3. Staff feel the scheme is having a detrimental rather than a beneficial effect; and

4. Quality control is not exercised over the operation of the scheme.

These issues must be addressed through careful planning and pilot testing, thorough briefing, comprehensive training and the systematic monitoring of the scheme in operation.

Developing the Scheme

Top management should drive the development programme, although the HR director can play an important part in gaining their commitment. Managers and staff should be jointly involved in developing the scheme, again with the support and advice of the HR function. This should be done through a working party, which has the responsibility for designing the scheme, and planning and executing its implementation.

Briefing

All concerned must be briefed thoroughly on the purpose of the scheme, how it operates, the part they will play and how they will benefit.

Monitoring and Control of Performance Systems

Training

It is essential to train everyone concerned in the operation of the scheme, i.e. both managers and their staff. Training should be given to them on how to set objectives, how to select and 'use performance measures, and how review meetings should be prepared for and conducted. Managers should be trained in counseling and coaching techniques.

Quality control

Quality control can be achieved by careful initial training, by managers' managers reviewing how performance agreements and reports are completed, and by the HR function monitoring the implementation of the scheme. Following the first complete cycle it is a good idea to conduct a survey of what both managers and their staff feel about how the scheme has worked.

Reliability and validity of performance appraisal

Some of the causes of performance appraisal ineffectiveness are problems that can affect the validity and reliability.

Validity problems are the halo effect, personal bias, central tendency, leniency and/or strictness error, overemphasis on recent behaviour etc. It has been experienced by many organisations that the tendency of the evaluator's to base assessments of all individual characteristics; on the rater's overall impression of the person being evaluated is halo effect. While individual characteristics are presumed to be independent of each other, yet a tendency to generalise from a predetermined overall impression can cause validity problems.

Sometimes, the appraiser may be biased because of regional or religious background, social or interpersonal conflicts and even personal values. Also, recent events are more likely to impress, while there is a tendency to forget or overlook more distant events. Also, there is a tendency to inflate ratings at sometimes, over times/or always in case of some rater's. There is a tendency to avoid using the extremes of rating scales and cluster the ratings around the midpoint. Leniency error results when evaluators artificially assign high ratings to all or a group of employees. In contrast, strictness errors result in artificially low ratings to all employees. Hence, there must be the highest standards of objectivity and an absolutely foolproof system.

Reliability ensures stability and consistency in the measurement. Inconsistencies among rater and instability over time can reduce reliability. Inconsistent use of measuring standards and lack of training in appraisal techniques also reduce reliability.

For instance, the content of performance appraisal must necessarily focus sharply on accomplishments, against performance objectives. A statement of objectives should reflect only those actions for which the individual has responsibility as well as control for achieving the results. Clarity of expression and behavioural specificity on the part of the evaluator is vital to motivate an employee to make an effort or the changes necessary to reach higher levels of performance, or even to maintain current effectiveness. Improvement needs should be linked with development needs and followup on development recondition is necessary, as failure to do so may de-motivate an employee.

Process of performance appraisal should ensure a good mutually satisfying relationship between manager and subordinate. One of the most powerful motivating influences towards maintaining or improving performance is selfesteem. Hence appraisals should be conducted in such a way that it either maintain or enhance the selfesteem of employees.

Every manager irrespective of his line and staff function is required to lead, guide, counsel and adequately motivate the team working with him to ensure successful achievement of the pre-set targets. Currently organisations are under tremendous pressure to get most out of their employees. A need for as effective performance management system is, therefore, the need for every organisation.

Performance management system (PMS) exhibits the following features:

- The organisation has a shared vision of its objectives, or a mission statement, which it communicates to all its employees;
- The organisation sets individual performance management targets, which are related both to operating unit and wider organisational objectives;
- It conducts a regular, formal review of progress towards these targets; . it uses the review process to identify training, development and reward outcomes;
- It evaluates the effectiveness of the whole process and its contribution to overall performance to allow changes and improvements to be made.

Some performance management systems place more emphasis than others on the opportunity they give for individuals to raise with their managers general questions concerning their work and aspirations. This can become a form of upward assessment in which individuals are encouraged to comment on any problems created by the ways in which they are managed and the resources made available to them; for example, the guidance and support they receive, the extent to which the authority they are given matches their accountability, or the facilities and equipment with which they are provided.

There are, however, certain characteristics, which are shared by all systems, which can truly be called performance management. These consist of the following:

- An agreement between managers and individuals on expected targets and/or standards of performance and other objectives. The agreement will aim to establish and/ or increase mutual understanding and to make clear the roles of managers and individuals in achieving targets and/

or standards or other objectives.

- A method of assessment of performance in relation to agreed targets and/or standards of performance and other objectives which is realistic and impartial. The assessment will aim to encourage individuals and their managers to exchange information, and com-ment on their achievements.
- A plan of action, which will enable individuals to make a new agreement with their managers. This might include:
  - A confirmation that targets and/or standards are being consistently achieved and remain appropriate;
  - The identification of improvement and/or development plans and methods for implementing them;
  - A Joint review of training or development needs and opportunities, and methods for satisfying them;
  - An opportunity for individuals and their managers to take a more general approach to the individual's position and role within the organisation. This may include the expression of aspirations, concerns and suggestions. It can, by mutual agreement, be informal and not recorded.
  - The operation of the system as a continuous cycle, starting with the performance agreement, covering objectives and improvement and development plans, which leads to the continuing review stage in which performance is reviewed informally as necessary and changes made to the performance agreement. This is followed by the preparation for review

stage during which the manager and individual separately prepare an agenda for the review meeting. Finally, the performance review meeting takes place at the end of the performance cycle when past performance is assessed and a view performance agreement is reached.

11

CONFLICT MANAGEMENT

Conflict is an important part of managing self. Conflict among individuals and between groups is a predictable and important part life. It can be personally and socially constructive, such as a focused debate on an issue that brings about increased growth in personal and social consciousness. A conflict becomes destructive when it destroys human dignity and degrades the values, ethics and life principles.

Conflict is an option, created by the choices you make. You always have the opportunity of choosing to choose again. Therefore, conflicts can be resolved by electing different choices with resolution so firmly in mind that it naturally leads to a shared vision of the future toward which to build. If you have to deal with other people, you will, sooner or later, have to deal with conflict. Conflict is not inherently bad. In fact, conflict simply stems from differing viewpoints. Since no two people view the world exactly the same way, disagreement is quite normal. In fact, anyone who agrees with you all of the time is probably telling you what you want to hear, and not what he or she actually believes.

The reason conflict has received such bad press is because of the emotional aspects that come along with it. When there is conflict, it means that there is strong disagreement between two or more individuals. The conflict is usually in relation to interests or ideas that are personally meaningful to either one or both of the parties involved.

REASONS OF CONFLICT

- Poor communication
- Seeking power
- Dissatisfaction with management style
- Weak leadership
- Lack of openness
- Change in leadership

CONFLICT INDICATORS

- Body language
- Disagreements, regardless of issue
- Withholding bad news
- Airing disagreements through media
- Conflicts in value system
- Desire for power
- Increasing lack of respect
- Open disagreement
- Lack of clear goals
- No discussion of progress and failure relative to goals, failure to evaluate the superintendent fairly and thoroughly or not at all

CONFLICT IS DESTRUCTIVE

Conflict is destructive when it:

(a) takes attention away from other important activities.

(b) undermines morale or self-concept.

(c) polarises people and groups, reducing cooperation.

(d) increases or sharpens difference.

(e) leads to irresponsible and harmful behaviour, such as fighting, name-calling etc.

CONFLICT IS CONSTRUCTIVE

Conflict is constructive when it:

(a) results in clarification of important problems and issues.

(b) results in solutions to problems.

(c) involves people in resolving issues important to them.

(d) causes authentic communication.

(e) helps release emotion, anxiety and stress.

(f) builds cooperation among people through learning more about each other.

(g) helps individuals develop understanding and skills.

POSITIVE AND NEGATIVE ASPECTS OF CONFLICT

Negative aspects of conflict are as follows:

1. It diverts time, energy and money away from the organisation's goals.
2. The situation can turn into continuous conflict.
3. It can adversely affect the health of the involved parties.
4. It can lead to sabotage, stealing, lying and distortion of information.

Positive aspects of conflict are as follows:

1. It usually causes changes.

2. It activates people.
3. It is a form of communication.
4. It can be healthy in that it relieves pent-up emotions and feelings.
5. It can be educational in that the participants often learn about themselves and the other people involved.
6. The aftermath of conflict can be a stronger and better work environment.

DIMENSIONS OF CONFLICT

Conflict describes as perception, feeling and action. It exists if at least one person believes or perceives that it exists and engages another in the conflict process whether the other shares the perception or not. Conflict is an emotional reaction to a situation or interaction that signals disagreement of some kind. The emotions felt might be fear, sadness, bitterness, anger or hopelessness. Unless conflict is externalised as action, it remains merely as an internal tension. It must be expressed or articulated. It can involve an attempt to make something happen at someone else's expense or it can be conciliatory, but the purpose is to get one's needs met. Another important point is that the feelings associated with conflict frequently diminish as people increase their awareness of the existence and nature of the dispute.

Conflict caused by Unmet Needs

The core of human conflict is human need. When people have needs that are not being met or needs that are inconsistent with the needs of others, they engage in conflict. Some of those needs are survival needs such as food, shelter, health or security. Some are based on identity needs, such as the need for community, meaning, intimacy or autonomy.

Conflicts in Interpersonal Relationships

Sometimes, in interpersonal relationships, such as those between you and one of your friends, there may be a conflict that you are not aware of. If someone who is normally upbeat and friendly toward you suddenly begins avoiding you or being rude, there is usually a reason. If the person has remained cheerful with everyone else except you, chances are you are dealing with a conflict situation. In these instances, you will want to address the problem by proceeding through the following steps.

1. Try to determine if there is a problem between you and the other person.
2. If you think there is a problem, set up a private face-to-face meeting to discuss the problem with the other person.
3. In a non-confrontational manner, ask the person if there is a problem. If his/her answer is "no," inform the person that you think there is a problem and explain what you think the problem is.
4. As you talk, ask for feedback. Do not "attack" the other person with accusations.
5. Try to listen to each other with open minds.
6. Be sure to respect each other's opinions.
7. Take a few minutes to recycle the other person's opinions in your mind.
8. Try to determine why the other person felt the way he/she did.
9. Avoid "finger-pointing."
10. Try to work out a compromise that pleases both of you.

Conflicts in Meetings

Conflicts in meetings can be very disruptive. But they can also be very helpful. Remember, conflicts are disagreements. If the person who is disagreeing with you is raising valid questions, it may benefit the group to address the issues they are presenting. In fact, by listening to them, you may gain valuable insight into what is and what is not working within your organisation. However, if the person continues past the point of disagreement to the point of disruptiveness, specific steps, like the ones below, should be taken.

1. Find some "grain of truth" in the other person's position that you can build upon.
2. Identify areas of agreement in the two positions.
3. Defer the subject to later in the meeting to handle.
4. Document the subject and set it aside to discuss in the next meeting.
5. Ask to speak with the individual after the meeting or during a break.
6. See if someone else in the meeting has a response or recommendation.
7. Present your view, but do not force agreement. Let things be and go on to the next topic.
8. Agree that the person has a valid point and there may be some way to make the situation work for both parties.
9. Create a compromise.

Conflicts in Negotiations

When you are negotiating with your clients, subordinates or even your friends, it is important to always keep in mind the idea that both parties are seeking a win-win situation. No one wants to feel like they are giving away something for nothing. In fact, most conflicts arise because one party feels like the other party is taking advantage of them. In order to avoid these types of situations, there are certain principles you can apply to increase your chances of a successful negotiation. These are as follows:

1. Avoid defend-attack interaction. It is non-productive every time.
2. Seek more information by ask a lot of questions.
3. Check understanding and summarise by making sure that you understand everything.
4. Try to understand the other person's perspective. Communication is more than just listening. Try to see it their way.

TYPES OF CONFLICT

Pseudo Conflict

It refers to those misunderstandings in which we perceive that there is a conflict when there is none. For instance, Rahul and Ramesh, may agree upon a topic but not realise this. They are interpreting one another's messages as being counter to their own messages.

This failure to understand and to realise their misunderstanding creates relational conflict.

Solution—Listen mindfully and check your perceptions with your partner. Try to avoid assumptions and mind reading.

Ego Conflict

This occurs when you are emotionally invested in a decision. We believe that if others disagree with us, they are rejecting us. Thus, we become stubborn, willful and proud.

Solution—Recognise that conflicts occur between the best of friends. No one will agree with another all the time. Disagreements are not an indication that the relationship is in trouble. Show grace if you have been obstinate and recognise that you have been wrong. Learn to apologise and to take responsibility for creating an ego conflict.

Simple Conflict

It is a difference of opinion that both parties recognise, acknowledge and accept. The conflict may be over how to share limited resources, whom to support in an election, or where to go for a dinner.

Solution—Agree to disagree in an agreeable manner. If the issue is minor, it is easier to compromise or accommodate. If the issue is major, it is better to collaborate to resolve the conflict.

Relationship Conflicts

These conflicts occur because of the presence of strong negative emotions, misperceptions or stereotypes, poor communication or miscommunication, or repetitive negative behaviors. Relationship problems often fuel disputes. Solution—Support the safe and balanced expression of perspectives and emotions for acknowledgment (not agreement). It is one effective approach to managing relational conflict.

Data Conflicts

These conflicts occur when people lack information necessary to make wise decisions, are misinformed, disagree on which data is relevant, interpret information differently, or have competing assessment procedures. Some data conflicts may be unnecessary since they are caused by poor communication between the people in conflict. Solution—Most data conflicts have "data solutions."

Interest Conflicts

These conflicts are caused by competition over perceived incompatible needs. Conflicts of interest result when one or more of the parties believe that in order to satisfy his or her needs, the needs and interests of an opponent must be sacrificed. Interest-based conflict will commonly be expressed in positional terms.

Solution—The parties must be assisted to define and express their individual interests so that all of these interests may be jointly addressed. Interest-based conflict is best resolved through the maximising integration of the parties' respective interests, positive intentions and desired experiential outcomes.

CONSEQUENCES OF CONFLICT

The consequences of conflict, whether positive or negative, are largely dependent upon the types of differences that lead to the disagreement. Disagreements among team members are bound to occur. But, so long as they focus on substantive, issue-related differences of opinion, they tend to improve team effectiveness. These types of disagreements are cognitive conflict. As team members gather to make important decisions, they bring different ideas, opinions and perspectives to the table. Cognitive conflict is beneficial because it requires teams to engage in activities that are essential for a team's effectiveness. It focuses attention on assumptions that may underlie a particular issue and which are often ignored. It improves the quality of team decisions.

MANAGING INTERPERSONAL CONFLICT

Conflict resolution can be a positive and constructive

social force. But it can also be used to avoid dealing with basic underlying problems and needs. At the base of many conflicts is an injustice. If conflict is resolved solely for the sake of harmony and at the expense of justice, the anger, resentment and frustration that fuel it can magnify and erupt into violence or other harmful manifestations. Premature reduction of confrontation may diminish volatility and bring about temporary comfort to persons involved. But in the long run, it can destroy the fabric of community and society.

Mechanisms of Conflict Management

1. *Negotiation*—It is a discussion among two or more people with the goal of reaching an agreement.
2. *Mediation*—It is a voluntary and confidential process in which a neutral third-party facilitator helps people discuss difficult issues and negotiate an agreement. Basic steps in the process include gathering information, framing the issues, developing options, negotiating and formalising agreements. Parties in mediation create their own solutions and the mediator does not have any decision-making power over the outcome.
3. *Arbitration*—It is a process in which a third-party neutral, after reviewing evidence and listening to arguments from both sides, issues a decision to settle the case. Arbitration is often used in commercial and labor-management disputes.
4. *Mediation-arbitration*—It is a hybrid that combines both of the above processes. Prior to the session, the disputing parties agree to try mediation first, but give the neutral third party the authority to make a decision if mediation is not successful.
5. *Community conferencing*—It is a structured conversation involving all members of a

community (offenders, victims, family, friends etc) who have been affected by a dispute or a crime. Using a script, the facilitator invites people to express how they were affected and how they wish to address and repair the harm that resulted.

6. *Peer mediation*—It refers to a process in which young people act as mediators to help resolve disputes among their peers. The student mediators are trained and supervised by a teacher or other adult.

PREVENTING CONFLICT

Most people have no interest in creating conflict with others. Most of us know enough about human behavior to distinguish between healthy communication and the words or actions that contribute to rocky relationships. It is in our interest to maintain relations which are smooth, flexible and mutually enhancing. The problem occurs when we fail to use cooperative approaches consistently in our dealing with others. We seldom create conflict intentionally. We do it because we may not be aware of how our own behavior contributes to interpersonal problems. Sometimes we forget, or we are frustrated and annoyed, and sometimes we just have a bad day. At times we feel so exasperated that we focus on our own needs at the expense of others. And then we find ourselves in conflict. To prevent conflict from happening in the first place, it is important to identify the ways in which we contribute to the disagreement. One way of doing this is to identify a specific, recent conflicted situation, recall what you said, and then think specifically about how you could have used more effective language. Think about ways in which your communication could have set a more trustful tone or reduced defensiveness. Then, once you have identified your part in the conflict, such as blaming, practice working on that particular behavior for a day or a week. At the end of the time period, evaluate your progress.

Effective Communication

Once you find yourself in a conflicted situation with someone else, it is important to reduce the emotional charge from the situation. This is to ensure that you and the other person can deal with your differences on a rational level in resolving the conflict.

Empathy

Try to put yourself into the shoes of other person. See the world through their eyes. Empathy is an important listening technique which gives the other feedback that he or she is being heard. There are two forms of empathy.

1. *Thought Empathy*—It gives the message that you understand what the other is trying to say. You can do this in conversation by paraphrasing the words of the other person. For example, "I understand you to say that your trust in me has been broken."
2. *Feeling Empathy*—It is your acknowledgment of how the other person probably feels.

Exploration

Ask gentle, probing questions about what the other person is thinking and feeling. Encourage the other to talk fully about what is on his or her mind. For example, "Are there any other thoughts that you need to share with me?"

Using "I" Statements

Take responsibility for your own thoughts rather than attributing motives to the other person. This decreases the chance that the other person will become defensive. For example, "I feel pretty upset that this thing has come between us." This statement is much more effective than saying, "You have made me feel very upset."

Stroking

Find positive things to say about the other person, even if the other is angry with you. Show a respectful attitude. For example, "I genuinely respect you for having the courage to bring this problem to me. I admire your strength and your caring attitude."

Rational Way of Resolving Conflicts

Identify the problem

Have a discussion to understand both sides of the problem. The goal at this initial stage is to say what you want and to listen to what the other person wants. Define the things that you both agree on, as well as the ideas that have caused the disagreement. It is important to listen actively to what the other is saying. Use "I" statements and avoid blame.

Come up with Several Possible Solutions

This is the brainstorming phase. Drawing on the points that you both agree on and your shared goals, generate a list of as many ideas as you can for solving the problem, regardless of how feasible they might be. Aim toward quantity of ideas rather than quality during this phase, and let creativity be your guide.

Evaluate these Alternative Solutions

Try to go through the list of alternative solutions to the problem one by one. Consider the pros and cons of the remaining solutions until the list is narrowed down to one or two of the best ways of handling the problem. It is important for each person to be honest in this phase. The solutions might not be ideal for either person and may involve compromise.

Decide on the Best Solution

Select the solution that seems mutually acceptable, even if it is not perfect for either party. As long as it seems fair and there is a mutual commitment to work with the decision, the conflict has a chance for resolution.

Implement the Solution

It is important to agree on the details of what each party must do, who is responsible for implementing various parts of the agreement, and what to do in case the agreement starts to break-down.

Continue to Evaluate the Solution

Conflict resolutions should be seen as works in progress. Make it a point to ask the other person from time to time how things are going. Something unexpected might have come up or some aspect of the problem may have been overlooked. Your decisions should be seen as open to revision, as long as the revisions are agreed upon mutually.

BIBLIOGRAPHY

Blake, R. and Mouton, J. S., *Solving Costly Organisational Conflicts: Achieving Intergroup Trust, Cooperation, and Teamwork,* San Francisco: Jossey Bass, 1984.

Brett, J. M., Goldberg, S. B and Ury, W. L., *Managing Conflict: The Strategy of Dispute System Design,* Business Week Executive Briefing Service, Vol. 6. 1994.

Brown, J. S. and P. Duguid, "Organisational learning and communities-of-practices: toward a unified view of working, learning, and innovation", *Organisation Science,* 1991.

Costantino, C. A., and Merchant, C. S., *Designing Conflict Management Systems: A Guide to Creating Productive and Healthy Organisations,* San Francisco: Jossey Bass, 1996.

Dana, D., *Conflict Resolution: Mediation Tools for Everyday Worklife,* New York: McGraw-Hill, 2001.

_____________., *Managing Differences: How to Build Better Relationships at Work and Home,* (4th Ed.). MTI Publications, 2005.

Daft, R. L. and R. H. Lengel, "Organisational information requirements, media richness, and structural design", *Management Science,* 1986.

Eby, L., "Collective orientation in teams: An individual and gruop-level analysis", *Journal of Organisational Behavior,* 1997.

Egger, E. and I. Wagner, *Time-management: a case for CSCW,* CSCW, ACM, 1992.

Ewing, D. W., *Justice on the Job: Resolving Grievances in the Non-Union Workplace,* Boston: Harvard Business School Press, 1989.

Furtado, T., *Why an Organisational Ombudsman? What an Organisation's Management Might Want to Know,* Dallas: Ombudsman Association, 1996.

Garbis, C. and Y. Waern, "Team coordination and communication in a rescue command staff: The role of public representations", La Travail Humain, 1999.

Hutchins, R. L., *Reprisal, Retaliation, and Redress: What an Organisation's Management Might Want to Know,* Dallas: Ombudsman Association, 1996.

McGrath, J. E., "Time, interaction, and performance (TIP): A theory of groups", *Small Group Research,* 1991.

_______________., H. Arrow, et al., "Groups, tasks, and technology: The effects of experience and change", *Small Group Research,* 1993.

_______________. and A. B. Hollingshead, *Groups Interacting with Technology: Ideas, Evidence, Issues and an Agenda,* Thousand Oaks, CA, Sage, 1994.

Sheppard, B. H., Lewicki, R. J., and Milton, J. W., *Organisational Justice: The Search for Fairness in the Workplace,* New York: MacMillan, 1992.

Slaikeu, K. A., "Conflict Management: Essential Skills for Health Care Managers", *Journal of Health Care Material Management,* Nov.-Dec.1992.

Vegt, G. V. D., B. Emans, et al., "Motivating effects of task and outcome interdependence in work teams", *Group & Organisation Management,* 1998.

Walsh, J. P., "Managerial and organisational cognition: notes from a trip down memory lane", *Organisation Science,* 1995.